I0096679

Axis Stone Mysteries

SUICIDE BLONDE

G. L. Keady

ALSO BY

G. L. Keady

DREAMRAIDERS

Sons of Steel Saga

FUTURES END
CYBERWARS
DARK ENERGY

First published in Australia in 2022
by Big Island Productions
Copyright © Gary Keady 2022

The right of Gary Keady to be identified as the moral rights
author of this work has been asserted by him in accordance
with the *Copyright Amendment (Moral Rights) AD. 2000*

This book is copyright.
Apart from any fair dealing for the purposes of private study,
research, criticism or review, as permitted under the Copyright Act,
no part may be reproduced by any process without written
permission.
Enquiries should be addressed to the publishers.

All rights reserved.

No portion of this work may be copied by any means without
prior written agreement of the publishers.

Big Island Productions
PO Box 3027, Tuross Head, 2537, NSW, Australia
www.bigislandprod.net

ISBN:
Ebook: 978-1-923038-09-7
Print: 978-1-923038-080-0

First edit by: Louise Falcioni
Print edit: Canon Doyle
Cover design and art: Brandon Evan-Keady

TABLE OF CONTENTS

CHAPTER ONE

THE NAME IS Stone... Axis Stone, occupation: private detective. You know, somebody says "follow that dude," so I follow him. Somebody says "find a missing chick," so I find her. And what do I get out of it? Fifty bucks an hour plus expenses. And if you think that buys anything fancy these days, then you're from outer space. It's a labour of love, but if I want to be honest, it's the only gig I feel comfortable doing.

You've probably heard about some of my cases on the news, but whatever you hear or read, the real thing is something else... and there's only one guy who knows that— I know it.

It was a stinking hot day outside. Sydney is like that in summer. But my office is cool— in both ways. The chorus to the song "The Terrible Tango" cranked up and cut through the tedium; it was the ringtone of my smartphone— one of my favourite tunes. I searched for the phone under a pile of unpaid bills and credit card demands piled high on my desk, found it, and put on my most congenial voice, hoping for a gig.

"Axis Stone Investigations, Stone speaking."

A silky, breathy voice at the other end purred, "Mr Stone, sorry, I'm out of breath. I was running to get out of the rain."

"Rain? You've got to be kidding!" I looked out of the window at the blue sky— there wasn't a cloud in it. "Are we on the same planet?" I challenged.

"Sorry, Mr Stone. I should have mentioned, I'm in Brisbane, and it's pelting down cats and dogs."

"I see, miss...?"

"Lola Lovejoy."

The name rang a bell. I'd seen it in the newspapers: nightclub singer Kitty Lovejoy kidnapped in some exotic place— yeah, the Philippines, that was it.

"Are you related to...?"

"Kitty? Yes, she's my sister."

"So, what can I do for you, Miss Lovejoy?"

"You know that she's missing in the Philippines. Well, we're having some difficulties dealing with the police in Manila, and the Australian Consulate there can only provide us with limited assistance and won't get involved in the kidnapping investigation."

"Yeah, that's the D-FAT policy as I understand it. So, go on... where do I come in?"

"My father is a prominent Brisbane identity and wants to keep our name out of the newspapers."

"Bit late for that, isn't it?"

"No more, I should say. What's been reported so far has already done some damage."

"So, what's the bottom line, Miss Lovejoy?"

"We need representation in the Philippines. Dad doesn't trust anyone there, so I contacted you."

"How did you find me?"

"On the net. Can you meet us in Brisbane for dinner tonight?" she asked tentatively.

"Email me an open-date return ticket and credit my account with three hundred bucks, and I'll be there."

~ ~ ~

The crud weather made the ninety-minute flight to Brisbane a turbulent affair, but nothing that a couple of in-flight JDs couldn't settle. I must admit I don't get to fly up front often, and I could get used to all the attention business class provided. I was seated next to a businessman who, by his demeanour and dress, made a living out of being a bore. He only spoke to me once during the flight, and his breath was so ripe I made sure there wouldn't be any more conversation by ignoring him. A sultry-looking girl with short dark hair and boobs about the size of tennis balls, the business class hostess, was pleasant enough, but that's about as far as it went— even that ended with her smile. She was a walking advertisement for braces— could eat an apple through a tennis racket.

I decided to kill time by mentally undressing the girl across the aisle. Evaluating people was one of my routines— especially pretty girls. In her mid-twenties with shoulder-length, well-groomed blonde hair, dressed in an A-line summery pale blue floral print number that showed off both her cleavage and her long, tanned legs, she was dressed to impress. The gold bangles on both wrists and the long, beautifully manicured fingernails told me she was a model. I followed the line of her shapely legs down to her shoes, unmistakably Jimmy Choo— expensive. She caught me looking and loved it; the edges of her sexy, red-painted mouth rose with a clipped smile. I immediately checked her ring fingers, knowing she would instinctively fiddle with them if she was already taken, but she wasn't wearing any. Instead, she reached down, and as though she was reading me better than I her, slipped off her shoes and began gently massaging her feet. Well, that pretty well did my head in— Mr Happy sprang into action, trying to fight his way out of my pants. So, by the time the plane landed at Brisbane airport, I was as horny as hell. As we deplaned, I got into position directly behind her and squeezed up tight enough for Mr Happy to rub into the cleavage of her lovely rear end. Again, she didn't mind at all and gently pushed her butt back to make better contact. I pulled out a business card and slipped it to her. She took it with a silent wink— pays to advertise.

~ ~ ~

Waiting at the airport cab rank, I was setting my wristwatch back an hour for daylight saving when, in my peripheral vision, I was struck by a pair of red Louis Vuitton open-toed high-heel shoes. I followed the shapely, tanned legs up to find a real honey: the sort you'd prefer to spread on a bed than on bread. A strawberry blonde garbed in a thin silk dress that clung to her slim, well-proportioned body like paint to a wall— only a wall is a flat surface. This dame even surpassed the blonde on the plane.

"Mr Stone?"

"All yours."

"Lola Lovejoy."

Her husky voice matched her name— Lola was a stunner— the gig was getting better by the second.

She lowered her Prada sunglasses for her wide-spaced blue eyes to meet mine. "I have a car waiting... follow me."

"No problem at all," I purred with a Cheshire cat grin.

The goods looked just as impressive from behind.

A dapper uniformed chauffeur held open the door to the white Mercedes C-class stretch limo, and I followed Lola inside. I sank into the plush leather seat opposite her, and she handed me an iPad.

"Here, everything you need to know, except your orders and payment details. We'll discuss those over dinner."

"Do I get to keep this?" I took the device and began reading.

"No," she said, crossing her tanned bare legs.

The next time I looked up, we were pulling into the driveway of a mansion.

"This your place?"

"No, Daddy's."

The Lovejoy estate was in immaculate condition. Trim green lawns ran off in all directions, neatly dotted with carefully shaped flowerbeds where all the flowers grew strictly to attention. The house itself was a rambling structure, maybe fifty years old, but it gleamed from the obvious and lavish application of care and money.

Unfamiliar with the high life, I felt like a fish out of water in the swanky dining room. A table set for three that could comfortably seat thirty-three. A butler with way too much starch in his shirt and the coat hanger still left in his suit coat showed me to a seat.

"Can I get you a drink, sir?" he said with a plum in his mouth.

It felt like a scene out of A Night at the Opera.

"Yeah, Jeeves, make it a Harvey Wallbanger." It was my preferred social drink.

"How's that, sir?"

I fired him a single raised eyebrow, figuring the recipe came with his suit. "Freshly squeezed orange juice, two fingers of vodka, a jig of Galliano, ice, a slice of orange only, no vegetation, and stir, don't shake."

"As you wish, sir."

"As I wish. If I'd known it was a wish, I'd have asked for three of them."

He ignored my wit and moved off stiffly. On his way out of the room, he passed an old guy suited up and balding, striding in as though he owned the place. He propped in front of me and offered me his hand.

"Mr Stone, Winston Lovejoy. Please, sit. Lola will join us directly."

"Nice pad you've got here, Winston. You're a high court judge, aren't you?"

"Yes, have you read the case file?"

"Ah ha, but I couldn't get the drift as to why Kitty was kidnapped and why there's been no ransom request."

"Now you can see our problem."

Just then, Lola floated in like on a cloud. The complete package: she could cause a room full of Parkinson's patients to stop shaking.

We stood for her to sit.

"Lola, Mr Stone was asking why there has been no ransom demand."

"That has us worried too, Mr Stone," she purred like a panther.

"Look, I've never been to the Philippines, so it's unfamiliar turf for me. The bottom line is, I make a practice of not biting off more than I can chew."

"We're not asking you to find Kitty, just monitor the investigation," Winston butted in, a little testily.

"If you find yourself in a position to rescue her, then fine, but that's not the brief," Lola calmly corrected.

"I see. This is because you're getting little from them?"

"Nothing would be more like it!" The old man cackled. I could see he was getting uptight. "Look, Stone," he snapped. "I've exhausted all my connections trying to get information, but we can't find out a damned thing!" His face had turned red, and he was puffing up like he was about to explode.

"Dad, take it easy, calm down. He has a heart condition. The stress of this is killing him. I'll take him up to his room; meet me in the drawing room. There's a bar there, help yourself."

She was speaking my kind of language. I watched her help the old boy out of the room, then went for a wander to find the drawing room and, more importantly, the bar.

A couple of minutes later, Lola was comfortably established in an armchair at one end of the fancy drawing room, a glass of Scotch in her hand, while I sat on a leather couch facing her, nursing a JD on the rocks.

She had changed her clothes. Whoever the guy was who created the silver lamé sheath she wore with such elegance was not only a master of design, I realized appreciatively, but also a miser with material. The sheath was sleeveless, and when she crossed her legs, the hem automatically hiked a good four inches above her knees. The entire creation was supported by fragile shoulder straps the width of her little finger, and the scooped neckline had the good taste to realize that even silver lamé couldn't compete with a substantial expanse of majestic cleavage and didn't try.

"Dad's aged since this all started with Kitty," she said dispiritedly.

"I can dig that." I got up and walked over to the open fireplace that wasn't alight. As a matter of fact, being in Brisbane, I wondered when it would be cold enough to light it. A mirror on the mantle caused me to assess myself. Short-cropped, mousey-brown hair that needed a trim, same for my three-day growth— reminiscent of Jamie Dornan, I thought, only after a big night out on the booze. Still, women love me, while most guys see me as a threat— anyhow, who gives a rat's? I repeat— women love me.

"See anyone you know, Mr Stone?"

I turned and faced her. "I see a guy with plenty to think about."

She took a sip of her Scotch, then shrugged her smooth bare shoulders in a quick movement, as if she wished she could shrug off any doubts.

"Oh, I think you'll make the right decision. You seem to be the kind of guy who embraces a challenge."

She got that right, the embrace part. I sat back down and drained my bourbon.

"Mind if I have a nightcap?"

She leaned forward in the chair and looked at me earnestly. "Help yourself, Mr Stone."

"Does that only go for the drink?" I quipped.

"It goes without saying that a man like you should know how to help himself, shouldn't he?"

"Comes with the license, lady," I said, pouring myself three fingers of rye.

"Is it fringe benefits you're inquiring about, Mr Stone?" she said pertly.

Returning to the couch, I declared, "If you don't ask, you don't get... that's my motto, Miss Lovejoy."

"Well, we might save that one until we know each other a little better," she sighed gently, tactfully sidestepping the innuendo of our little tête-à-tête. She placed her glass, still half-full as I would see it, on the coffee table and then stood with great poise.

"Your bedroom is the first left on the upstairs landing. Breakfast on the balcony at 8 A.M., sharp. You'll find pyjamas on your bed and all you need in the en-suite bathroom. Goodnight, Mr Stone."

"Right." I shot her a grateful smile. What a broad, I mumbled to myself.

CHAPTER TWO

TWO DAYS LATER, I was sipping champagne in first class on a Qantas flight from Sydney to Manila. I had arranged to be collected at Manila airport by a local private investigator named Ricky Esposo. I found him at arrivals holding a card under his chin with my surname on it.

We got to know each other as we crawled through the infamous Manila traffic en route to my hotel in Makati. I hadn't seen traffic like it before. Ricky was a stocky little bloke with a razor-sharp wit, and we hit it off immediately.

He drove his late-model white Corolla up to the fancy entrance of the Shangri-La Hotel, and I was impressed. It was a top-shelf joint— little guys in white uniforms surrounded the car to open doors and take my bags. I felt like King Farouk. After I checked in, I took Ricky up to my room to discuss the case, and it didn't take me long to realize how switched on he was— I guess it comes with the territory.

"So, Ricky, what's the scoop on the Kitty Lovejoy fiasco?"

"Well, Mr Stone, there's not much to tell. She came to Manila a year ago, contracted as a lounge singer at the Captain's Bar in the Mandarin Oriental Hotel— the top lounge bar in the Philippines. That's where she met Buddy Nelson, the American owner of Dawn Talent Agency in Makati. He provides plenty of artists work in television commercials and local movies, as well as booking singers into a number of clubs. He got her plenty of work. Filipinos like her sexy movie star look. She starred in a few notable television commercials, and then she got a residency at 71 Gramercy Bar Lounge in Century City, the numero uno upmarket nightclub in Makati."

"Was that through Nelson as well?"

"Don't know, boss. After that, she was in all the social pages a lot with known local gangster Ringo Raye. He owns Gramercy."

Ricky handed over his iPhone. "Here's the venue poster."

I checked the photo— a hot redhead in a slinky red evening dress that titillated the imagination, standing on stage next to a grand piano. Then it struck me like a ton of bricks.

"That's Lola!"

"No, boss, that's Kitty."

"She's got a sister. They must be identical twins..."

I needed to check out the abduction details. Ricky had all the newspaper articles, but I wanted to hear from someone closer to the victim. Ricky suggested Kitty's personal assistant, a Filipina with the unusual name of Chiki Dee. He took me to her condo in Fort Bonifacio, a suburb of Makati.

~ ~ ~

Ricky waited in the car while I rang the intercom. After I explained myself, a husky, sexy, accented voice invited me up. The apartment door opened to a cute little suntanned thing in a pink robe.

"Hi, are you Chiki Dee?"

"Chiki Dee," she purred. "Please come in, Mr Stone."

It was a small, modern apartment with scant furnishings. She sat on the three-seater lounge and drew her legs up. The front of her robe inadvertently dropped open enough for me to catch sight of a lovely breast. She caught me looking and quickly closed the gate.

"How can I help you?" she said, curtly.

"I understand you were with Kitty when she was abducted."

"Yes, we were in the Century City car park after the performance when..."

She burst into tears.

I leapt out of the armchair, sat beside her, and placed my arm around her shoulders to comfort her, like every white knight is supposed to.

"Calm down... it's okay to tell me. What happened in the car park?"

She sniffled. "Oh, we were walking to the car when two masked men came out of the dark, pulled a hood over Kitty's head, and pushed her into a waiting car. Before I could do anything, they sped out of the car park."

"COVID masks?"

"No, hoods."

"Okay, anything about them you recognised?"

"I don't know, Mr Stone. I'm very afraid," she said, teary-eyed.

I dropped the subject to help settle her down and started talking about herself. She opened up.

"Are you from here, I mean Makati?"

"No, I'm from Bicol in the province."

"Is that a town?"

"No, Legazpi City is the town."

"How long have you been in Makati?"

"For nearly seven years now. I've been with Kitty as her PA for a year. Before that, I was two years with EDSA Shangri-La public relations, and before that, I finished a Bachelor of Communication at Eastern University in Manila, which took four years."

"Clever girl. Your family must be very proud of you. Did you leave your hometown to attend university?"

"Um," she looked sheepish. "I'll be honest with you, I got into a little trouble at home, which meant I needed to leave town."

"Oh, can I ask what that was?" I thought it might have something to do with Kitty's kidnapping.

"I got pregnant by a local boy. I was only just eighteen."

She hopped up, went to the bedroom, and returned with a framed photograph, handing it to me. It was of her and a young boy.

"My son Carlo, taken last year. He was six then."

"A good-looking lad. So, is he in Bicol?"

"Yes, with my parents and my ten brothers and sisters."

"Ten! Is your father a primary producer?"

"No, he works at the council," she said, not getting the joke. "I have been saving my money to send Carlo to a good school... education is very expensive in the Philippines, you know."

"Don't you have public schools here?"

"Yes, but there are so many children that there is no chance. If you want to get a start in life, you must go to a good school, and that will cost nearly one hundred thousand pesos a year."

"About two grand US. I guess that's a lot of money for you?"

"Yes. I saved up a deposit from working. It took me three years, but now I have enough to get him enrolled. I am going to Bicol in two days to pay the deposit."

"So, you must be worried about Kitty. Your savings must depend on having a job."

"Yes, it does, sir."

"Help me find her, Chiki. Do you know this guy, Nelson?"

"Yes, he's not a good man."

"Hmm, I see. Tell me something about what happened, anything."

She pulled a face like she was about to cry and pleaded, "But I don't know anything, sir, honest."

I got up. "Okay, look, you have a think about it, and I'll come back tomorrow at the same time, and we'll talk some more."

She shot me a warm smile as I left her with a gentle peck on the cheek, as every white knight should do.

I climbed into the front seat of the car and woke up Ricky.

"Hey, sorry, Ricky. I got carried away."

"No problem, boss," he yawned. "Did you learn anything?"

"Yeah, plenty. She's afraid to point the finger at the kidnappers but knows something. I'll need to coax it out of her. We'll come back at the same time tomorrow."

"The storm has passed," Ricky said, looking up at the rolling clouds. "We get one of those every day this time of year. It's the rainy season."

He drove me back to the Shang. It was late, and I was beat. Before I got out, I asked him, "I'll need a gun, Ricky."

He produced a holster and gun from under the seat.

"Thought you'd ask. Here, but be careful, boss. Everyone in Manila carries a loaded gun— they shoot first, ask questions later."

"Sounds dangerous."

"It's still a cowboy town... well, that's what a Yankee private detective once told me."

"I like you, Ricky. We'll make a top team. Go home and get some rest. Do you start early?"

"Not really, boss... but..."

"A man after my own heart. Meet me at 8:30 A.M., by the pool for breakfast."

I watched the Corolla snake down the driveway, and then I headed into the Shang. The busy lobby was filled with eye-candy. It seemed to be the place for Manila socialites to strut their stuff at that time of night.

International hotels are weird. The lobby is always bustling, but you rarely see anyone in the corridors. I always fancied that one day I'd step into an elevator and find a honey to die for, on her own, just hanging for a sexual fling for the night. I suppose it's a bit like wanting to be seated next to a sex siren on an international flight— you know, she's on her way to a porno convention in Miami or somewhere and wants to join the mile-high club for bragging rights before she gets there. But hell, with all the fights I've taken over the years, I'm still a mile-high virgin.

CHAPTER THREE

RICKY JOINED ME poolside for breakfast. "Morning, boss."
"Sit down, Ricky. I've ordered you coffee."
"Salamat po."
"What's that mean?"

"Thank you in Filipino," he said brightly. "Tagalog."

"Cool, keep teaching me. It'll be good to learn something more than swear words in a foreign language," I joked.

"Okay, boss... So, where to today?"

"Our first stop will be Mr Nelson at the Dawn Agency."

It was tough leaving the beautiful bodies in their string bikinis lazing about in deckchairs by the pool like lounge lizards, but I had crooks to catch. Besides, I was sweating up a storm, and carrying a pistol meant I couldn't take off my sports coat.

Ricky waited in the car while I went inside the Legazpi Village office building. Ignoring the four flights of stairs, I took the elevator. Even then, by the time I reached the cute receptionist, my armpits were leaking like a faucet. The air conditioning was a relief.

"Hi, honey. I'd like a word with Buddy Nelson," I said.

She stood up, and I gave her a quick once-over. She was short but well-endowed, a cute thing with blue and green streaks in her long black hair.

"Who's calling, sir?" she whispered, fluttering her eyelashes.

I gave her my best profile and huskily announced, "Axis Stone, private detective representing the Lovejoy family."

She disappeared behind a partition, then returned moments later to usher me into Nelson's office.

Nelson was a large man with a receding hairline and a gnarly face underlined with jowls. He offered me his big mitt to shake.

"How can I be of assistance, Mr Stone?" he said in a southern USA accent.

"I presume you're up to speed on the Kitty Lovejoy kidnapping. I have a few questions."

"Fire away."

"Where were you the night she was taken?"

"I was at dinner with an actress... Why? Am I a suspect?"

"Just clearing your name... Any idea why she was kidnapped?"

"Try asking her boyfriend, Ringo Raye."

He was giving me bad vibes, not to be trusted. "You sound like you've got a bone to pick with Raye."

"You could say that. He stole one of my stars."

"Hmm, I see. Tell me something, where are you from?"

"I live down the street... Are we done with the questions?"

"Cute," I said, standing up and eyeballing him. "Don't try to hardball me, Nelson. I've got a .45 in my desk drawer to take care of vermin like you. We're done."

"For now, Nelson... With your attitude, I'd say you're from Louisiana."

"What's that supposed to mean, Aussie?"

"You said it in one, Nelson. How did Raye take your star when you didn't even get her the Gramercy gig?"

I didn't wait for a reply. I thought I'd leave him with that thought and bail out.

On the way out, I gave the sexy receptionist a wink. By her response, I got the impression I was a big hit with the local talent. I wondered if that was normal in this town for a reasonably young, virile, handsome foreigner.

When I got into the Corolla, I had to wake up Ricky. I don't know how he can sleep in the car, but I guess it's the air conditioning.

"Where to now, boss?" he mumbled sleepily.

"I want to talk to the cop in charge of the investigation."

"That would be Sancho Cortez. He's the principal investigator for Task Force Shanghai."

On the way there, I decided to pick Ricky's brain a little.

"Hey, listen, it seems I'm getting attention from young, pretty Filipinos."

"You mean Filipinas, boss."

"Yeah, is that normal for a guy like me?"

"They probably think you're Hugh Jackman, boss. That's why girls here would be attracted to you."

"Hugh Jackman, huh? Hmm, Wolverine," I said, leaning back in the front passenger seat, feeling pretty good about myself. "Yeah, yeah, I can see that."

We parked in San Antonio and walked the short distance from the car park to Police HQ.

"I wasn't impressed with Nelson. Take a look in his closet, Ricky. See if you can dig up any skeletons."

"Will do, boss. I know Cortez... He's a tough one. He won't like a foreigner snooping around his case... Be careful, boss."

"I hear you, Ricky. But don't worry, I know how to handle cops with a chip on their shoulder. It happens a lot back home. It's an occupational hazard."

"Not like this, I think, boss."

We received a cool reception from the Desk Sergeant when I asked for Cortez. He kept us waiting for an hour before finally calling us into his office. Thank heavens they had air conditioning, or I would have passed out.

Cortez glared at me from behind his desk, as if I were the next item up for auction that he had no interest in. No formalities.

With a snarl on his rugged face, he declared, "I have no time for foreigners sticking their nose into police business."

We sat. He reminded me of Eli Wallach, who played Tuco, the cool bad guy in the classic '60s spaghetti western "The Good, the Bad, and the Ugly." I decided to give him a taste of his own medicine.

"Is coming to talk to you sticking my nose into your business?"

"You've got five minutes, Mr Stone."

"The Lovejoy family wants an update on the kidnapping. They're not getting anything from you, so they sent me over."

He lit a half-smoked cigar and blew smoke in my direction. It stank.

"We haven't heard anything. No ransom demand. Forensics combed the crime scene and found nothing. The only witness won't talk."

"You mean Chiki Dee?" I croaked, coughing from the smoke.

"You've done some homework, at least. I'm impressed," he said cynically.

He was small in stature but, like Ricky, a tough nugget. He had medium-length black hair parted at the side, with a couple of long bangs that draped down over his left eye. He had a take-no-prisoners look in his eyes, an acne-scarred face with a constant scowl, as if someone had pinched his lunch money— uncannily Tuco.

"Suspects?" I asked.

"Only one: Ringo Raye."

"Motive?"

"The girl was cheating on him."

"You mean Kitty?"

"Yeah."

"Do you have any proof of that?"

"I have no reason to doubt it, but no proof either."

"Did she mention anything about Raye's criminal activities?"

"No."

"Was it difficult for her to break up with him?"

"Put it this way, he's not the sort of guy who easily accepts being dumped. He has a huge ego."

"Were there any repercussions?"

"More like an undeclared war."

Raye was shaping up to be the villain. I downed what I could of my drink without poking my eye out with a celery stick.

"Thanks, Cortez... Sorry for the interrogation, but we're on the same side here."

He flicked my card back to me.

"Call me if you hear anything," I said.

He glanced at it, then dropped it irreverently on his desk. "I don't have the budget for making long-distance calls, Stone."

"My local mobile number is on the back. I'm staying at the Shangri-La."

"I know, room 677," he said smugly, a reminder that I was in his town, on his turf.

"Drop in, and I'll buy you lunch."

"Okay, I will consider it."

"Is it fine with you if I have a word with Raye and Vargas?"

"Be my guest. Goodbye, Mr Stone... Ricky."

As we made our way out of the door, he called out, "Stone, two things you should know. One, you shouldn't be carrying a gun without a permit. And two, be very, very careful. This isn't Sydney, di ba?"

"Have you ever seen 'The Good, the Bad, and the Ugly'?" I countered and didn't wait for an answer.

On our way back to Makati, an idea struck me.

"Ricky, where can we find this Nicholas Vargas guy?"

"Probably at the Manila Yacht Club."

"Good, let's go there for lunch."

"But you're not a member, boss."

"Don't worry, I bet Vargas is. The traffic was so bad that it took us an hour to reach the classy club on Roxas Boulevard, facing Manila Bay. Ricky wasn't convinced about getting us in, but I enjoyed the challenge and had confidence in myself. I guess I lost him when I told him earlier that I knew how to handle cops. Boy, did I get that one wrong with Cortez. I had to regain his trust.

We walked into the lobby, and I confidently approached the receptionist. With my best debonair voice and a confident smile, I said, "Good afternoon. I'm here to meet Nicholas Vargas the third."

"Your name, sir?"

"Mr Lovejoy."

"For a while, sir."

She waddled off, presumably to check with Vargas. A few minutes later, she returned with a handsome, suave, and sophisticated-looking guy, whom I guessed to be in his mid-thirties. He left her and confronted me.

"Mr Lovejoy, Nick Vargas."

We shook hands. The guy was smooth and polished. He even vaguely resembled George Clooney.

"Is there somewhere we can have a drink and talk?" I asked.

He nodded, and we headed to the bar. The view of Manila Bay through the huge floor-to-ceiling windows was spectacular.

"Can I buy you both a drink?" Vargas asked in a well-educated manner.

"I'll have a Harvey Wallbanger, and Ricky?"

"Super Dry, boss."

Vargas led us to a window table.

"So, Mr Lovejoy, I presume this is about Kitty?" he asked.

"Sorry for the masquerade, Vargas, but the name is Axis Stone. I'm a private detective from Australia representing the Lovejoy family. This is my associate, Ricky Esposo."

Ricky shook Vargas's hand.

"I expect the cloak and dagger charade is appropriate considering the circumstances. How can I help?" Vargas said casually, unaffected by my little game.

I could see why women would fall for this guy. He had it all—money, status, looks, savoir-faire. And he was as smart as a whip. I instantly took a liking to him. He wasn't flaunting his graces and airs; he was genuine.

"My shout," I said.

Vargas smiled gracefully. "No can do. House rules. Only members can buy drinks. What will it be?"

"I'll have a Harvey Wallbanger, and Ricky?"

"Super Dry, boss."

Vargas led us to a window table.

"So, Mr Lovejoy, I presume this is about Kitty?" he asked.

"Sorry for the masquerade, Vargas, but the name is Axis Stone. I'm a private detective from Australia representing the Lovejoy family. This is my associate, Ricky Esposo."

Ricky shook Vargas's hand.

"I expect the cloak and dagger charade is appropriate considering the circumstances. How can I help?" Vargas said casually, unaffected by my little game.

I could see why women would fall for this guy. He had it all—money, status, looks, savoir-faire. And he was as smart as a whip. I instantly took a liking to him. He wasn't flaunting his graces and airs; he was genuine.

"My shout," I said.

Vargas smiled gracefully. "No can do. House rules. Only members can buy drinks. What will it be?"

"I'll have a Harvey Wallbanger, and Ricky?"

"Super Dry, boss."

Vargas led us to a window table.

"So, Mr Lovejoy, I presume this is about Kitty?" he asked.

"Sorry for the masquerade, Vargas, but the name is Axis Stone. I'm a private detective from Australia representing the Lovejoy family. This is my associate, Ricky Esposo."

Ricky shook Vargas's hand.

"I expect the cloak and dagger charade is appropriate considering the circumstances. How can I help?" Vargas said casually, unaffected by my little game.

I could see why women would fall for this guy. He had it all— money, status, looks, savoir-faire. And he was as smart as a whip. I instantly took a liking to him. He wasn't flaunting his graces and airs; he was genuine.

"My shout," I said.

Vargas smiled gracefully. "No can do. House rules. Only members can buy drinks. What will it be?"

"I'll have a Harvey Wallbanger, and Ricky?"

"Super Dry, boss."

Vargas led us to a window table.

"So, Mr Stone, how can I help you?" Vargas asked.

"Well, I wanted to ask you a few questions about Kitty's kidnapping."

Vargas leaned back, sipped his drink, and sighed. "I'm really worried about Kitty. If there's anything I can do to help, just let me know."

"Do you have any idea who might have kidnapped her?"

"My best guess would be Ringo Raye."

"And why do you say that?"

"Because Raye went public, claiming that Kitty was his girlfriend, and then lost face when I came along. It seemed like he was stalking her rather than being in a genuine relationship."

"Stalking her? That's a serious accusation."

"She wanted nothing to do with him once she learned about the true nature of his business. At first, she thought he was just a nightclub owner, but it didn't take her long to realize that nightclubs were only a cover for his criminal activities."

"Involved in the drug trade, perhaps?"

"I have no reason to doubt that, but no concrete proof either."

"Did she ever mention anything about that to you?"

"No."

"Was it difficult for her to break up with him?"

"Let's just say he's not the type of guy who easily accepts being dumped. He has a huge ego."

"Did she face any repercussions?"

"It was more like an undeclared war."

Raye was shaping up to be the prime suspect. I finished what I could of my drink without poking my eye with a celery stick.

"Thanks, Nick. Sorry for the third-degree, but we're on the same side here."

Vargas handed me his business card. "Call me if you need any further help. I really care about Kitty."

"I will. Thank you."

We left the club, and as we walked through the car park, I asked Ricky, "What do you think of our friend Nicholas Vargas?"

"He's a straight shooter, a good man to have on your side, boss."

"An honest trader, huh?"

"Yes, and I think he genuinely cares about Kitty. He'll help if you ask him."

"Got that impression. It's good to know that money talks the talk in this place. Take me to Chiki Dee's apartment."

~ ~ ~

We pulled up outside the Fort Bonifacio condo.

"Call it a day, Ricky. I'll find my way home after talking to Chiki."

"Okay, boss..."

"The next step will be to speak with Ringo Raye. Can you arrange that?"

"Hmm," Ricky pondered the idea. "That might take some doing, boss."

"Let's meet at 8 A.M. by the pool for breakfast again, and we'll see how you've got on."

"Okay, boss. Do you have pesos for a taxi?"

"Yeah, I've got a couple of thousand. Is that enough?"

"It should only cost two hundred and fifty pesos. It's not far from here to the Shangri-La. Any more, and the cabbie is ripping you off."

"Cool bananas! Catch you later, Ricky."

I climbed out of the car, glad to have Ricky on my side, and went up to the apartment intercom. Someone was coming out, so I slipped inside through the open door.

But as I reached the apartment, my gut twisted. Something was terribly wrong. The door was wide open. I pulled out my gun and cautiously entered. A quick scan of the living room revealed no sign of Chiki.

"Chiki! Are you there?" I called out, tentatively.

I checked the bedroom—nothing. Then I entered the en-suite bathroom and found Chiki perched naked on the toilet, her head tilted back, and her throat slit from ear to ear. Her naked body was drenched in blood. She had been murdered, and it seemed recent.

"Ah, Chiki, why?" I mumbled regretfully. I holstered my gun and backed out of the room, being careful not to leave any footprints in the large pool of blood on the tiled floor.

Suddenly, I felt the prod of cold steel in my back. A voice shouted, "Hands in the air... real slow!"

I complied, raising my hands.

"Look, I'm a private eye. I found her like this," I tried to explain.

Then the lights went out.

CHAPTER FOUR

I **WOKE UP** with a pounding headache in a putrid police cell, covered in filth. A bump at the back of my head made it clear that I had been hit hard. Just as I was getting to my feet, the cell door swung open, and two officers rushed in. They each took an arm and forcefully escorted me up a hallway into a harshly lit interrogation room. At the very least, it didn't reek like the cell. I was tossed into a chair.

"Your ID says Axis Stone, private detective from Australia," said one of the cops, his stern face mirroring his rank, visible by the pips on his shoulder strap.

"So, you can read. That's a good start. What am I being charged with?" I grumbled, deciding to play on the defensive.

"I didn't say you could speak," he retorted, hitting me on the side of my head, causing my left ear to ring.

"Hey, cut the physical! My embassy will hear about this..." I started.

"Shut up! What were you doing at Dee's apartment?"

"Can I answer?" I asked.

"Yes, that was a question."

"She's a friend. I was visiting."

"And why did you cut her throat?"

Suddenly, I felt very uncomfortable. Being accused of a murder I didn't commit in a foreign country was something I had only seen in documentaries. The possibility of being locked up indefinitely was becoming very real.

"Look at me," I showed him my hands. "Do you see any blood? She was killed by a knife, for Christ's sake. It's clear I didn't kill her! What would be my motive? And why did the police arrive just after me? Was there a tip-off? It's a setup, and you know it."

"That's for us to determine, Stone. Lock him up," he ordered.

They hauled me back to that repugnant cell. An hour later, they released me without any explanation. I collected my belongings - a wallet, now devoid of cash, my smartphone, and naturally, not my gun.

Disgusted and smelling like rotting seafood, I caught a cab to the Shang. I was savvy enough to stash a twenty-buck note in my shoe for emergencies, so I managed to cover the fare.

It was a relief to return to my room. I immediately stepped into a scorching hot shower to wash off the foul smell of the prison. Just as I was lathering up, a loud knock echoed through the room. Annoyed, I quickly wrapped myself in a robe. The knocking became increasingly aggressive. "Alright, alright, keep your shirt on," I yelled.

Opening the door, two intimidating figures pushed their way in, forcing me onto the bed at gunpoint. "Hey, what's going on?" I asked, bewildered.

A sharp-dressed man with a trendy haircut and an expensive suit walked in behind them. They set a chair in front of me for him. Some sort of royalty, maybe?

"Your reputation precedes you, Mr. Stone," he said, with a refined accent — another mestizo like Vargas, but a bit rougher around the edges and certainly shadier. He had the cold eyes of a shark, reminding me of a sleazier version of Christian Bale.

"Yeah, and to whom do I owe the pleasure?" I asked.

"Ringo Raye. Pocket the hardware, boys." At his command, his thugs put away their guns and I allowed myself to relax a fraction.

"Why the dramatic entrance, Raye? You could have called first," I grumbled.

"I thought I had the right after paying a thousand bucks to bail you out of jail," he replied coolly.

Clearly, this man had serious connections. I was locked up for murder, and somehow, he managed to get me out. What a system.

"Why'd you cut me loose?" I asked, trying to match his threatening tone.

"Because I'm being blamed for a kidnapping I didn't commit. Next, it'll be Dee's murder. I thought, after your experience with local law enforcement, you might be willing to cooperate, especially since you owe me."

"Listen, Raye, I didn't ask to be bailed out, so let's just call it even," I said defiantly.

"Not in my town, Stone," he responded, his voice icy. "Listen carefully. You're either with us or against us. Believe me, you don't want to be my enemy."

His warning was crystal clear, and he certainly wasn't just blowing hot air.

I pushed him further. "Who kidnapped Kitty?"

He lit a cigarette, ignoring my objection about the smoking restriction on this floor.

"Three possibilities. Vargas wants me gone. Cortez wants to put me behind bars and might use Kitty to do it. Nelson's desperate for money and would do anything to get out of debt. Take your pick," he replied.

"Let's start with Vargas. Are you her boyfriend or is he?" I asked.

"I am. Why else would I make her the star of my club and publicly announce that she's my girl?" he responded, irritation flaring in his eyes.

"And does she feel the same way?"

He fiddled with one of his many rings, a telltale sign that he was about to lie. "Yeah, if Chiki had lived, she could've confirmed that. But someone made sure she wouldn't talk, didn't they? Did you ask her about me?"

"Hmm, I guess you're right. No, I didn't ask her about you. What about Cortez? What's his issue with you?"

"He blames me for his brother's murder."

"And did you kill him?"

"No, his brother was an undercover cop who got killed in a drug bust. What can I say?"

"That leaves Nelson. What's his story?"

"Like I said, he's a desperate low-life. He'd do anything to get out of debt."

"Isn't that the pot calling the kettle black?"

"Watch your mouth, Aussie," he warned, shooting me a stare that sent chills down my spine. I knew I should've dropped the sarcasm, but I couldn't resist one last jab.

"Then maybe aliens abducted Kitty. Because there's been no ransom demand, and that's not normal."

Raye gave me a long, menacing look. "I've made my case, Stone. Now do your job. If you need some muscle, call me."

He handed me my phone that had been confiscated by the police. "Tito, give him his piece," he ordered.

Tito handed me my gun and holster. Raye stood up. "No hard feelings, even left it loaded. Now that we're acquainted, whoever it is, aliens or otherwise, I want them caught, and I want Kitty back."

"You run this town, Raye, why don't you find her?"

"Too much heat," he muttered, heading towards the door. "My number's saved on your phone under 'R'. Oh, and your friend Ricky Esposo has been texting you. You should let him know you're alive."

With that, he and his goons exited, leaving me to call Ricky and fill him in.

I was tired and was about to hit the sack when there was another knock at the door. My first thought was, "Not again." This time I went armed but didn't need to open the door; I found a note sticking out from under it. I yanked the door open and checked the corridor, but there was no one. I went back inside, sat down, and read the note. Then, I rang Ricky and read it to him.

"It says for me to go alone to the Star Bar in Quezon City at midnight tonight and ask at the bar for Zorro... for fifty thousand pesos I will learn where Kitty Lovejoy is. What do you think, Ricky?"

"I think it's what you say: bull's shit."

"That's bullshit, Ricky."

"No, I mean it."

"Yeah, yeah, I know... but why would somebody go to all the trouble of delivering me a note at the hotel if there's nothing to it?"

"That's what they want you to think. It could be anyone who knows about the case — all they want to do is to rob the foreigner."

"What time is it?" I mumbled, checking the room clock. "Half past ten."

"You're not really thinking of going, are you, boss?"

"What are your plans for the evening, Ricky?"

"I gotta drop some money off to my family in Diliman."

"Is that anywhere near this Quezon City?"

"Yes, it's in Quezon City."

"How about you drop me at the Star Bar on the way?"

~ ~ ~

I cashed a thousand US dollars in traveller's checks at the cashier, which got me a little over fifty grand in pesos. It sounded like a lot. I thought, "Shit, if I cashed all my bucks into pesos, I'd be a millionaire."

I waited for Ricky to pick me up, and then we headed for Quezon City. The traffic wasn't bad, and forty minutes later, we pulled up outside the tiny nightclub. It was just before midnight.

"You ring me and I will pick you up, boss. I'm only fifteen minutes away. You sure you don't want me to come with you?"

"No, it's okay. If you don't hear from me by 1 A.M., bring the cavalry."

"I hope you didn't bring your gun."

"Not that silly, Ricky," I chuckled, getting out of the Corolla. If he only knew I was that silly. There's no way I was going to waltz into the Star Bar on my own, unarmed. I watched Ricky drive off and then headed for the front door, which was dressed up in fairy lights like Christmas.

Disco music from the seventies was pounding... it felt like I'd entered a time warp. A solitary mirror ball suspended from the ceiling was firing stars everywhere in the room and animated the half dozen couples grooving on the dance floor. A bar stretched along the back wall of the otherwise dark, unembellished room — black walls, black floors, black tables, and chairs. Not a lot of imagination had gone into the decor. There were four or five patrons on stools at the bar, all of them staring in my direction. I felt like they were sizing me up as if I'd just arrived from outer space. However, attention has never ruffled my feathers, so I headed for the bar. I pulled up a bar stool and waited for the barman to work up the courage to approach me. He got in front of me and then just stared blankly, so I took the initiative.

"Give me a Jack Daniels and coke." I wasn't game to ask for a Harvey Wallbanger, not in this hole. You never know what you'd get.

"Sorry, sir, only beer."

I looked at all the spirit bottles decorating the shelves on the wall behind him and pointed at a bottle of Jack.

"What's that, di ba?" I thought to throw in a bit of Tagalog I'd learned, to help.

He grabbed the bottle and showed it to me. It was empty. He waved his hand at the rest of them.

"All gone."

I got it... empty was the word he needed — they were only for show.

"Okay, I'll take a San Miguel super dry."

He brought me a bottle and no glass.

"How much?"

"Twenty-five pesos."

I slipped him a hundred pesos bill. But before he could take it, I held it down on the bar top with my index finger.

"Where's Zorro?" I bargained.

He pursed his lips and pointed his chin in the direction of a door at the back. I wouldn't have made it out if it hadn't been for the mirror ball illuminating it just in time.

"Keep the change," I said, generously. The tip was about a buck and a half. I took my beer and cruised over to the door. Before I knocked, I looked back at the barman. He was on the phone, I guessed, with Zorro. It didn't surprise me when the door jerked open without me knocking, but it did surprise me who had opened it. She was wearing a thigh-length black robe - she swivelled on a dime and led the way into a dimly lit room.

"Take a seat, Mr. Stone," she said huskily. "I'm glad you could make it."

I sat in the armchair in front of the desk and put my bottle of beer on it. "Well, let's see if coming all this way has been worthwhile. 'Are you Zorro?'"

"Yes, did you bring the money?"

There was only a desk, a couch, and a chair in the small office room with a single lampshade in the corner for light. She was tall for a Filipina, with long shiny black hair, shapely legs, tanned skin, and exotic looks. But the light cast a certain shadow on her face that made her look suspicious. She sat on the edge of the desk and lit up a cigarette.

"Do you smoke?" she asked, her voice feminine yet husky.

"Socially unacceptable these days... Look, I'm all for public relations but what have you got to tell me?"

"Are you in a hurry, Mr. Stone?" she inquired, abruptly.

I shrugged. "Not really, but it's getting late, and it's a long way back to Makati."

She took a long draw on her cigarette and the glow at its tip lit up her mysterious eyes. They almost squinted.

"What do you know about Kitty Lovejoy?"

She got up from the edge of the desk, casually discarded the cigarette on the floor, extinguished it under her black high-heeled pump, and then floated behind the desk like a stripper about to start her act. She had me intrigued. More so when she pulled a gun out of the top drawer and pointed it at me.

"Put the money on the desk, Mr. Stone."

CHAPTER FIVE

I **WAS ANNOYED** it had come to this, but deep down, I had anticipated it. There I was with a gorgeous, seductive woman, my hands raised in surrender.

"The money is down the front of my pants, and I should warn you, I don't wear underwear."

"Don't be smart, Mr. Stone," she retorted coldly.

Keeping her gun trained on me, she strolled around to the front of the desk and used the barrel to flick open my jacket. After a thorough inspection to ensure I wasn't armed, she nodded. "Reach into your pocket and retrieve the money. No tricks, Mr. Stone, or you'll get shot."

I believed her. So, I slowly reached inside my jacket, conscious that my .38 was tucked in the back of my pants, and pulled out the wad of notes. I handed it over to her.

"So, does this mean you're only robbing me, and there's no information?"

She didn't respond but instead cautiously retreated behind the desk and hit a button on the hands-free phone module.

"I hope you realise, of course, that I wouldn't have come here without informing the cops. If I don't appear out front at 1 A.M., they'll tear this place apart looking for me."

The door swung open, and two menacing-looking thugs charged into the room. She instructed them in Tagalog, and they each grabbed one of my arms, hoisting me from the chair.

"Pleasure meeting you too," I grumbled at her.

They manhandled me through the club in a big hurry, with no one paying any mind. I didn't make it easy for them, forcing them to drag me rather than walk.

Outside, they bundled me into the back seat of a dilapidated old cab and wedged themselves on either side. Unexpectedly, one of them pulled out a stiletto blade and flaunted it. I got the message. My .38 was a nagging presence in my back pocket, but I needed to choose the right moment to use it. The driver fired up the engine and we lurched off. The guy without a knife decided then was a good time to land a punch in my gut.

The pain in my stomach had subsided to a dull ache, one I might recover from in a couple of years. There had been no conversation since we left the Star Bar, and I was craving the sound of a human voice.

"Listen, I paid fifty thousand pesos for this ride. You could at least take me to my hotel."

I received another brutal punch in the solar plexus in return. Now I understood why it's called the solar plexus; you see stars when someone hits you hard enough there.

I was starting to sweat from the lack of air conditioning when a car screeched from nowhere, swerved right in front, and cut us off. Our driver hit the brakes to avoid a crash, and we hit the curb with a jolt and stopped. A gun barrel then tapped on the side window.

The voice behind the gun yelled out, "Labas!" The two thugs sensed the intensity of the order and obeyed promptly. As the door opened, I could see Ricky in the headlights of his Corolla, his gun trained on the two thugs.

"Dapa!" He barked.

They hit the deck, arms outstretched.

Casually, Ricky leaned inside the car. "You okay, boss?"

"You call this a taxi ride without air-con?" I joked with the cabbie. The old man was shaking like a leaf. I got out and slid into the Corolla. Ricky got behind the wheel, and we drove off.

"Thanks, Ricky... You didn't go home, huh?"

"No, boss. I thought it best to wait outside the Star Bar for you."

"Lucky you did. I think I was being taken for a one-way ride."

"You mean lucky I woke up... I was asleep. They probably wouldn't have killed you anyway, boss, just stick you with a knife and leave you in the boondocks bleeding."

"Lovely... the lack of air-con was torture enough."

"They weren't pros," he added.

"How could you tell?"

"They were scared out of their wits."

I leaned back in the seat and yawned. "Okay, let's go visit your folks."

"No way, boss. First, we need to get your fifty thousand back."

~ ~ ~

We pulled up outside the Star Bar.

"You said you're not armed, but I think you are, boss," Ricky observed, a mischievous grin on his face.

"That's what I like about you, Ricky. You see right through me."

"Okay, I'm experienced with situations like this, so leave it to me. But have your gun ready."

"I hear you," I responded, exiting the Corolla, relieved for Ricky to take the lead.

"Stay close," Ricky instructed before dashing into the club and heading straight for the bar. The dance floor was deserted, and only two customers sat at the bar – the same bartender serving as before.

"Is that him?" Ricky asked, pointing at the bartender.

"Yep," I confirmed, my tone gruff.

Ricky squeezed between the two customers, his threatening gaze making them both uncomfortable. He growled, "Vamoose!" They took the hint and bolted out of the club, leaving the bartender frozen in place. Ricky asked him calmly, "Where's Zorro?"

The rat-faced bartender shrugged, feigning disinterest. Ricky beckoned him closer to whisper something. Expecting a bribe, the bartender leaned in. Suddenly, Ricky seized his arm, hauling him onto the bar. He writhed on his back like a captured mackerel until Ricky grasped his throat. The thrashing stopped.

"Where is she?" Ricky demanded sternly.

Terrified, the bartender pointed a shaky finger at the office door.

"Is that where you went before, boss?"

"Sure is," I affirmed.

Ricky glared at the bartender then shouted, "Get out!" Getting the message, the bartender was yanked from the bar, landing hard on the floor. He scrambled up and bolted from the Star Bar.

With guns drawn, we approached the office door like a SWAT team on a TV show. At Ricky's nod, I kicked the door open. We rushed in, guns at the ready, with me aiming at Zorro behind her desk, and Ricky targeting a large man seated in front of her. They both jumped to their feet, startled by our intrusion.

Without a word, Ricky rushed the large man, gesturing with his gun for him to sit back down. The gun pressed to his head ensured he didn't resist.

"Put your hands up and move them away from the desk, Zorro!" I commanded. "Where's my money?"

"He's got it!" she retorted, pointing at the large man. "I just paid off my debt with it."

Ricky wasted no time, pressing his .38 harder against the man's temple and cocking the trigger.

"The money, where is it?"

"Pocket," the man grumbled.

"Hand it over. Try anything, and I'll paint the wall with your brains."

He complied, hastily digging into his side pocket and nervously retrieving a roll of notes. Ricky snatched it from his hand and tossed it to me. I counted out fifty grand and threw the excess on the desk.

"There's enough left to pay off your debt. It's yours if you tell me what I want to know."

With her hands in the air, she sighed and rolled her eyes.

"What's your real name?" I demanded.

She glanced at the money on the desk, then back at me, pondering her options. Cautiously, while keeping a wary eye on the large man, she said, "Rita Gutierrez."

"Who set you up? Was it him?" I pressed.

Ricky jabbed his gun even harder into the man's temple.

"No! No! No!" she protested. "It has nothing to do with him. I heard about it, did some research, and figured I could make the money I needed."

"Very enterprising of you, Rita, but you picked the wrong mark," I said, satisfied with her story.

In the car en route to Diliman to visit Ricky's family, I posed a question to him. "Do you think she was telling the truth?"

"I don't know, boss. I can't believe a woman with her looks needs to pull a stunt like that to make money. I think there's more to it than meets the eye."

"I'm with you on that, mate. It felt like a set-up to me, a distraction. As if someone was trying to either scare the crap out of me or put me off the scent."

"Maybe both, boss."

"I think you're right. Have you heard that name before, Gutierrez?"

"It's a common name here in the Philippines."

"Well, I'll just add it to my list of interest-bearing grudges."

Ricky found that amusing, but to me, the list was palpably real.

We paid a brief visit to Ricky's family home in Diliman. By Filipino standards, it was a close-knit, small family. Ricky's younger brother worked in the States. Both parents, in their mid-seventies, struggled with health problems — the father with Parkinson's disease and the mother with osteoarthritis. Yet despite their challenging afflictions, they were in high spirits, elated to see their son and warm toward his foreign friend. The purpose of our visit was for Ricky to provide some financial support. I admired Ricky's devotion to his folks. That night, my estimation of him grew substantially.

On our drive back to the Shangri-La, I asked Ricky about his parents' pension. He confirmed they received one, but it only amounted to three hundred pesos per month each — equivalent to six US dollars. Hardly enough to feed a dog. I started to empathize with these people for whom poverty was a way of life. The society was class-stratified with a vast population of the very rich, a small middle class, and the rest — the masses. With an average monthly wage of merely two-hundred and seventy-nine US dollars, it's little wonder life is cheap. Ricky informed me that a staggering six percent of the Philippine economy is owned by two ethnic Chinese business magnates with a combined net worth of nearly fourteen billion US dollars. This place was steeped in corruption. I started to think that the Philippines' history of being occupied by numerous nations over centuries hadn't given its people the chance to develop individuality, a sense of self-worth. Initially, they were Malay tribes infiltrated and assimilated by Muslims in 5 A.D. Then the Chinese came, integrating with the indigenous population and have continued to do so since. In 1591, the Spanish conquered and colonized them, followed by the British in the 16th century, then America in 1898 until 1933 when the Japanese ousted the Americans. In 1942, the USA returned to displace the Japanese and reoccupied the country from 1945 until 1992 when they finally withdrew their military forces. No wonder these people suffer from an identity crisis; they haven't a clue who they are.

Changing the subject, Ricky asked me, "You seemed attracted to Zorro, boss."

"Yeah, I don't know, Ricky," I responded, "there's just something about an attractive woman with a gun in her hand that gets my adrenaline going."

"That could be a dangerous habit," he remarked, flatly.

"You hit the nail on the head there, buddy-boy," I conceded. "Women have been the bane of my existence ever since I can remember."

"Do you lose it when you get horny?" he probed.

"Put it this way, one whiff of those female pheromones and rational thinking flies right out the window."

"I'll try to remember that in the future," he chuckled.

"Are you implying I messed up with Zorro?" I queried.

"Just an observation, boss," he responded.

"Tell me more," I said.

"You were armed, and yet you allowed her to take control of you. You could've gotten both of us killed," he pointed out.

"I hear you... I hear you," I admitted. The truth always stings, especially when someone you hardly know gets a read on you. My one fatal flaw had been exposed again, and I had been lucky to escape intact — when will I ever learn? Sounds like a Pete Seeger song.

By the time Ricky dropped me off at the Shang, it was nearly 3 A.M. We agreed to meet by the pool at eight in the morning. I dragged myself up to my room, so exhausted that I fell into the sack still dressed.

CHAPTER SIX

I WAS BUSY taking in the eye candy on show in and around the Shang pool when Ricky rolled up.

"Morning, boss."

"Park your bod, Ricky. What's up?"

"Word is out on the street that the cops are gunning for you."

"The cops, hey? Why's that?"

"Cortez wasn't told about your arrest or release until after the fact. I think he knows who bailed you out."

"Yeah?" I glanced at him over my Ray-Bans. "Well, if Raye's word is gospel, then Cortez would think I've pitched in with the guy. It makes perfect sense he'd come after me. Someone murdered Chiki and then called the cops to set me up. The question is: how did Raye know I'd been arrested?"

"You suspect him?"

"Right now, I suspect everybody except you and I, and even thou art a little dubious."

"What do you mean, boss?"

"Nothing, it was just a joke."

The Terrible Tango played. I flashed Ricky the caller ID: Lola Lovejoy. He nodded. I stood up, took the call, and talked while pacing up and down poolside.

"Hey Lola, what's up? You have? What! So, it was a guy... any accent? No, right... Did you speak to Kitty? Hmm, okay... you what?... in the background? Yeah, that might mean something. No, don't do anything, let me mull it over, and I'll get back to you. I'm making a little headway here. It won't be long before we get a break. Okay, bye."

I hung up and returned to Ricky. "Big news, there's been a ransom demand. A guy with a disguised voice phoned the Lovejoys and asked for two million US in crypto to be transferred to a numbered account within forty-eight hours. He threatened to cut off one of Kitty's fingers each day until he gets the lot."

In the old days, ransom was paid with bags of cash: notes were traceable by numbers, dye, or later GPS homing microdots on individual bills. Now it's a digital transfer of crypto to a numbered account and virtually impossible to trace. Technology took the edge the good guy once had and handed it over to the crooks.

I sat back down, deep in thought.

"What are you thinking, boss?"

"Lola said she could hear lapping water and birds in the background. What does that tell you?"

"A boat, the beach, a lake... a resort hotel."

"I'll need a safehouse, Ricky. Can you arrange one? No, better still, here," I handed him my phone. "Ring Cortez, I should confront him before this gets out of hand."

While Ricky spoke Tagalog to the police operator, I paced about, weighing up the options. The question of who killed Chiki and why bothered me. Now that the kidnapping was about money, the plot had thickened. The question was— which suspect needs that much dough and knows the family well enough to be confident of getting it? Who has the readies and the savvy to set up an offshore numbered bank account? You'd think that would eliminate Cortez, leaving Nelson, Raye, and Vargas. Would Vargas need money? I don't think so, he's already loaded. My bet was on Nelson, though Raye is such a cunning operator he couldn't be discounted. Which one of them knew I would visit Chiki?

"Boss, Cortez will meet you."

The rendezvous was set for Café Breton in the outdoor plaza section of Greenbelt: a large modern shopping mall in Makati not far from the Shangri-La Hotel.

~ ~ ~

We found Cortez under an umbrella at a table in the alfresco section of the popular café.

He looked up at me with piercing eyes. "Stone, I selected a neutral location as a sign of good faith."

"I'm impressed," I said, pulling up a seat opposite him, as did Ricky.

It was close to lunchtime. I checked the menu.

"The Excalibur looks good. Are you eating, Cortez?"

"You paying?" he asked.

"Yeah." I handed him the menu.

"What were you doing at Dee's apartment?" he questioned nonchalantly while studying the menu.

"Getting her to talk about the kidnapping," I returned serve.

He lowered the menu and eyeballed me. "Did you kill her?"

"Now that would have been pretty stupid of me, wouldn't it? No, don't be ridiculous."

He handed the menu to Ricky.

"That's what I thought. So, who set you up then?" Cortez asked coldly. "And who bailed you out, and why?"

I was pondering whether to tell him about the ransom demand.

"I'll tell you what, let's exchange some home truths. Agree?"

The waiter arrived.

"I'll have an Excalibur and an iced vanilla latte. How about you, Cortez?"

"A Neptune and a short black."

Ricky added, "Make that two."

"Okay, Stone, what have you got?"

The passing parade of sexy ladies was distracting for me, but I managed to decide what to focus on.

"Firstly, yes, Raye bailed me out, but you already know that, don't you? I have no idea why or how he even knew I'd been arrested. Secondly, there has been a ransom demand."

Cortez sat forward in his chair with a look of intrigue on his rough dial. "When?"

"This morning... Two million US in crypto to a numbered account within forty-eight hours."

"That changes everything. All right, Stone, now that there has been a demand, we will need to be on the same page. I'll come clean with you. You were not set up by the police; someone dialled 117. Vargas, Raye, and Nelson are my three main suspects, but there is a fourth."

The food arrived, momentarily distracting us.

"A fourth, you say?"

"Yeah, the fiancé of Nick Vargas... Bianca Gutierrez: a socialite gold digger who didn't take too kindly to being dumped by him for Kitty Lovejoy."

Bells were ringing for Ricky and me. We exchanged a quizzical look.

"I see the name means something to both of you," Cortez said perceptively.

"We had a bit of a run-in last night with one Rita Gutierrez, alias Zorro."

"Ha!" Cortez chuckled facetiously. "That cheap hustler. She's a relative, runs a cheap bar in Quezon City."

"The Star Bar," Ricky said.

"Yeah, that's the one. Did she try to blackmail you or something?"

"You could say that," I said.

"That's her form," Cortez almost sang. "What about this Bianca Gutierrez? Is she made of the same stuff?" I probed.

"A class act but still with a bad streak," he confirmed.

"Runs in the family," Ricky scoffed.

"Why's that?" I asked.

"She was probably the meal ticket to her family," Ricky chimed in. "Their one big chance for getting into the elite old-money set through Vargas."

"Wouldn't be the first time a spurned jealous lover took revenge in this town," Cortez observed, chewing his sandwich.

"Why the ransom?" I posed.

"Money is everything in Manila," Cortez admitted, "and they would have the means to set it up."

"By 'they,' you mean the Gutierrez family?" I questioned.

Cortez was growing on me... he had dumped the arrogance and lightened up.

"They'd stop at nothing to get rich," he chuckled.

For the first time, I noticed his gold front tooth. It made him look even more like Tuco.

"Ricky, I'd better meet this Bianca Gutierrez."

"I'll set it up, boss."

"Tell me how it turned out with Zorro?" Cortez asked with a cynical smirk. "From memory, she's quite a dish."

"Let's just say I'm putting it down to experience," I said smugly.

Cortez shot me a cynical smirk. "A close encounter of the Filipina kind. There'll be more of those before you're through here, Mr Stone. Just make sure you count your fingers after you've dabbled."

Over lunch, we resolved to keep on the same page. Cortez would focus on Dee's murder, while I'd continue interviewing suspects. Sooner or later, we expected a break in the case, but the clock was ticking.

Ricky dropped me at the Shang, and after some research, I made a conference call to the Lovejoys.

"Lola, Winston?"

"Hello, Stone. We're feeling a little more confident after the ransom demand," Winston admitted gruffly. "At least we now know where we stand."

"True. I checked the account. It's a hole-in-the-wall bank in St. Vincent, West Indies, impossible to access."

"Can we put someone there to watch for a withdrawal?"

"No, Winston. It's crypto. From there, it will almost certainly be automatically bumped from one crypto exchange to another until it's eventually remotely collected from goodness knows where."

"So, what should we do then?" Lola asked, emotionally.

I suggested tentatively, "Locate her inside the time limit."

"And if we fail?" she questioned.

"Then she loses a digit. Look, the kidnapper wants money. He's not going to harm her. It would mean dealing with a hysterical hostage and managing a nasty wound—that's just not on."

Winston snapped, "Are you suggesting we call his bluff?"

"Oh, please give us a better alternative than that?" Lola pleaded.

"Okay, pay the two mill, get her back, and then with her help, we'll track down the kidnapper. That's my advice," I said unyieldingly.

It was no surprise when they chose the payout option, and that translated to a totally different approach from our end. The handover would be tough with no assurances that after the ransom is paid, the kidnapper will surrender the hostage—he might simply ask for a second dip. We needed to make a counterproposal to prevent that from happening, but without direct contact with the kidnapper, we'd have to wait for his next call, and that would mean possibly missing the deadline and risking Kitty losing a digit. I phoned Cortez.

"I've spoken with the Lovejoys, and they're willing to pay up. Yes, no assurances. We could go to the press with a counteroffer to attract the kidnapper's attention. Say—Ransom demand made for Kitty Lovejoy—family will pay but first need release assurance. Good, I'll leave it up to you to run it. We need to devise a release and arrest strategy. Okay, my hotel room, 9:00 a.m. tomorrow."

I hung up and immediately got a call.

"Stone speaking... Ringo, what's up? Tonight, out front of the Shangri-La at ten. What's this about? Okay, done."

Raye had something to tell me in person, cloak and dagger stuff I know, but that's how it was going to be played out from now on. I was thinking about hitting the swimming pool when Ricky rang. He'd set up a meeting with Bianca Gutierrez at Café Havana in Greenbelt. I knew it was right next door to Café Breton. I'd scoped it out when we had lunch with Cortez. We agreed to meet there at 6 p.m. I decided to use the spare time for some research on the net.

~ ~ ~

It was only a short walk from the Shang to Café Havana, but at that time of day, the footpaths were so crowded I ran late. Fortunately, Ricky had gotten there early and grabbed a table in the alfresco section.

Café Havana is more a bar than a café. It offers small Spanish Tapas dishes and an extensive drinks menu. A popular happy hour hangout, it was my kind of joint. Gutierrez hadn't arrived, so I ordered our drinks.

I told Ricky, "Ringo Raye phoned, wants to meet tonight."

"Why?"

"He wouldn't say over the phone. He'll pick me up at ten."

"You might need me along, boss?"

"Nah, I'll be okay. Either he's trying to bond with me to get some dirt on a suspect, or he's planning to take me for a ride."

Shaking his head, Ricky said, "Boss, you can't trust anyone in this town, especially you... a foreigner! They'll knock you over just like that!" He clicked his fingers.

The click rang home—life could be snuffed out that easily here. I must admit, after what happened to Chiki and my time in that stinking cell, along with the Star Bar treatment, I was inclined to take notice of Ricky's warning. I don't think of myself as a slow learner, but something was telling me I needed to meet with Raye.

The drinks arrived. I had taken a punt on a Wallbanger, and compared to the last effort at the Yacht Club, this one had had a haircut—far less vegetation—but it had one of those little umbrellas that I immediately flicked. The place was filling up fast, and the scenery was first class. I was glad mandatory COVID mask-wearing was done. Too many not-so-good lookers had been taking advantage of the cover—eyes had become more alluring during that time. There were lots of long suntanned legs and plunging necklines at Café Havana, and the girls looked sexy as well. Huh! only joking.

Ricky's phone rang. I looked up and sighted the most gorgeous babe I'd seen since meeting Lola and Zorro heading our way. On the phone, she waved at Ricky. Wow! I figured Kitty must be something special for Vargas to have dropped this stunner. I stood to greet her.

CHAPTER SEVEN

"MISS GUTIERREZ I'M Axis Stone. Please sit," I gestured.

She sat and daintily crossed her long, shapely, light brown legs. At five-eight, she was tall for a Filipina, and though a better sort than Zorro, there were similarities. Wearing a designer white satin blouse with a plunging neckline that had my imagination screaming for more—a sleek light brown knee-length skirt, she reeked high-maintenance. I recognised the bag on her arm as a Gadino, retailing for around forty grand US—then there'd be little change from a grand for her beige Christian Louboutin high-heeled sandals. Tasteful accessories: a Cartier Crash watch, no rings—a pair of diamond stud earrings, a carat apiece, Carven sunglasses, and her shiny long black hair worn up, which showed off her jawline and lovely neck to perfection. I'd learned to read threads and accessories from my mentor, DI Malone of CID Sydney. He taught me they were the best window into the personality of any male or female.

"You want to ask me about Nicholas? I was in the area, so I agreed to meet you. Otherwise, I wouldn't have bothered," she snarled arrogantly, with pouted red-painted lips.

Boy, this bird had the temper of a rabid dog. Made me wonder if she just had a distaste for foreigners or if she was a genuine twenty-five-year-old Y-gen snob.

"I'm glad you bothered coming; you've brightened up my day," I said with my best smile that generally works to lighten things up.

"Well, I'll be, a gentleman. Guys like you are a rarity these days," she quipped.

"Well, thank you, Miss Gutierrez. May I call you Bianca?"

"No! My friends call me Bee."

The ice had broken, maybe because she'd picked up that I fancied her.

"So, Bee, did Ricky mention what I do?"

"You're an Aussie private dick retained by the family of the red witch."

"You mean Kitty?"

"Call her what you like, but red witch is a more accurate description of the bitch."

There was obviously no love lost between them.

"Do you have any idea who kidnapped her?"

"No, but they get a standing ovation from me."

"I see... so tell me what happened when Vargas broke up with you?" I asked, ignoring her angst.

"Now, that one will cost you a drink."

"Certainly, I'm sorry... what will it be?"

She lowered her sunnies and peered over the top of them with a dreamy squint, "A flute of French champagne, of course."

This broad would be more expensive to run than a Bugatti Veyron, and I know which I'd prefer, though she sure has bedroom eyes.

Ricky signalled a waiter and ordered.

"It was my idea to see the red witch at Gramercy. Our friends had seen her perform and were impressed. We, that's Nick and I, had been an item for a year and were planning on getting married mid-next year. He'd met Ringo Raye at a casino. I expect you know all about him? He was the red witch's lover—it was all over the social pages."

Bee Gutierrez wasn't about to pour her heart out; she was way too tough a broad for that.

"Raye brought the witch over to our table after her set."

"Why?"

"To show her off, I guess. He's like that. Seems Nick was more impressed with her than I first thought because two weeks later, he told me it was over between us."

"Didn't give you a reason?"

"Just said he'd realized marriage wasn't right for him now. I, of course, said fine, let's just wait. But he said he needed a break from our relationship and was planning a trip to the States... to think. Later, I found out he didn't have plans of going there unaccompanied."

"Kitty?"

"You got it in one... my, aren't we clever? Now, where's that Goddamned drink!" she barked like a spoilt brat.

Her Gadino handbag burst into song with "Shake it Off" by Taylor Swift. She whipped out her phone and checked the caller ID.

"I need to take this," she said curtly.

She got up and walked around behind me to take the call. Within seconds, she was shouting at the phone in Tagalog. I couldn't understand what she was saying, so I whispered surreptitiously to Ricky.

"Who's she arguing with?"

"Her brother."

"What about?"

"Sounds like he doesn't approve of her being here."

Her voice was full of raw emotion. Then the argument stopped—she returned and flopped into her seat, fuming. Her demeanour had reshaped to accommodate her petulance. I sensed she was about to cut out, but I needed more answers and was saved by the late arrival of her flute of champagne. After a sip of it, she calmed down some.

"I'm sorry... that was my brother, Arnel."

"That's okay, is everything all right?... You look..."

"Sometimes he comes on too strong with the big brother crap," she growled.

By the intensity of the argument, it seemed more than that to me, but I let it go.

"So, did Nick go to the States with Kitty?" I asked her.

"No, but it didn't end there. My parents wouldn't accept that after they'd given Nick permission to marry me, he'd renounced it. So, they took it up with his family and the Church," she said, with a catty expression that wasn't becoming at all.

Before she could utter another word, just as she was taking a sip of champagne, someone pushed through the crowd and smacked the flute out of her hand. It shattered on the pavement. I jumped up. The assailant grabbed Bee by the arm and tried to forcibly drag her away from our table, both of them screaming in Tagalog.

I grabbed the guy by the shoulder and shouted, "Hey fella, let her go!"

He took a swipe at me... I saw it coming, swayed, and his fist grazed my chin. Instinctively, I returned serve with a right jab that I landed right on the button. He went down like a bag of potatoes. You'd think Bianca would appreciate being rescued, but no, she turned on me and let fire with both barrels.

"You've killed my brother, you monster!"

A flurry of punches followed that were more threatening than her brother's. Fortunately, Ricky came to the rescue, grabbed both her arms from behind, and whispered in her ear in Tagalog to calm down. I checked her brother. He wasn't knocked out, only dazed with a bleeding nose and a split lip.

Two security guards appeared out of the crowd and helped him up. He was a good-looking young guy, even with a bloody face. A mestizo: half-Spanish and Filipino, shorter than me, under six feet, early thirties, wiry but cut, dressed in designer jeans and a polo shirt.

A guard stood between us to keep the peace.

"Come on, Bianca, let's go!" he growled angrily, trying to pull away from the guard's grip.

I hollered at him, "That's no way to treat your sister!"

Still restrained by the guard, Arnel got in my face.

"Stay away, foreigner, or you'll wind up in a freakin' body bag!"

Constraining Bianca, Ricky chimed in. "Watch your mouth, Gutierrez!"

"Let go of me!" Bianca shouted, then pulled away from Ricky and hit him with a brutal verbal spray in Tagalog. By the look on Ricky's face, it wasn't very lady-like. With her anger vented, she grabbed Arnel by the arm and dragged him off into the passing throng. The guard let me go, and I sat back down at the table.

"What did she say to you, Ricky?"

"Ah, just a childish threat, boss."

"Nothing's childish, my friend. I now rate those two right up there on the list of suspects, capable of anything. If my instincts are correct, then this isn't the end of it; he'll retaliate. Dig up what you can on him. I've got a gut feeling about him—crap seems to run in their family."

"You think he's the kidnapper?"

"No, but he stinks of complicity."

"Are you all right, boss?"

"Yeah, Ricky, he only grazed me. Anyhow, let's check the menu. I'll buy you dinner, mate."

Ricky studied it.

"I should take you for Sisig, boss."

"Yeah, what's Sisig?"

"Filipino delicacy."

"If there's no rotten fish or offal in it, then I'm up for giving it a try, buddy."

Ricky laughed.

"No worries, boss. Nothing rotten and no guts."

~ ~ ~

We walked through Ayala Center, which was packed with a plethora of people and loads of pretty ladies all very pleasing on the eye. We got to mall Glorietta 5, made our way to the 2nd floor, and entered Gerry's Grill. Ricky managed to get us a table even though the restaurant was full.

I sank into a wicker chair and studied the menu.

"I'll order Filipino delicacies for you," Ricky said, with a cheeky grin on his face.

The waitress arrived, and he spoke to her in Tagalog, so I had no idea what he was ordering until he got to the drinks, and then I recognised the words, "super dry." The appetizers arrived quickly, one sizzling and smelling great, the other a little suspect.

"Try this first," Ricky said, pointing at the sizzling dish.

I tried it, and it tasted fine.

"You like it?"

"Yeah, it's all right," I said as the beers arrived.

"Okay, try this one."

As I raised the spoon with what looked like little fish on it to my mouth and it smelt putrid... it tasted how it smelt, gross.

"Ew!" I shrieked, gagging on it. I quickly threw down half a bottle of Super Dry to kill the taste. "Man, that is wrong, what the stuff is it?"

"Green mango with Bagoong... fermented fish."

"Man, I said nothing rotten... you can include me out of that one. What's the other one?"

"Sizzling Balut with Tofu."

"So, what's Balut?" I asked, hesitantly.

"Sure you can handle it? You ate it."

"Oh no, don't tell me I just ate something rancid?"

"Duckling foetus," he mumbled, tentatively.

"Hmm, well I can just about handle that."

"We normally drink it down raw while it's still inside the egg."

I took another big swig of beer to wash it all down. Three more dishes arrived. The first two didn't look too offensive, but the third looked like shrivelled-up spiders.

"What the stuff's that?" I exclaimed.

"Crunchy squid heads," Ricky said, with a big smile. He picked up a couple and chewed them up. "Hmm, very good... come on, try, boss."

I wasn't about to be outdone and scooped up a bunch of them, bravely shoved them in my mouth, and munched them up. I stopped chewing with a frozen look of terror and watched Ricky sink in his chair, then I relaxed my face into a smile and happily announced, "Excellent!"

Relief broke on Ricky's face. The other two dishes were sizzling pork sisig and sizzling seafood gambas, both culinary triumphs. I wasn't sold on the Bagoong or the Balut, but the other dishes were exceptional. The bill arrived; it was one thousand and twenty pesos: ten bucks US each—unbelievably cheap. Ricky was stoked that I'd enjoyed some of his country's traditional dishes, and I was happy to add them to my culinary database.

~ ~ ~

By the time I arrived back at the Shang, it was almost time to meet Ringo, so I waited in the lobby. It seemed that at ten on a Friday night, there's a change of guard in Makati. The day-trippers clock off to bed, and the night prowlers' surface to strut their stuff. A row of international clocks on the wall backing reception all said it was time to be picked up, so I wandered out onto the forecourt. Filipinos are not noted for their punctuality due to the malignant traffic congestion. Well, that was the excuse anyway, but Ringo's mob seemed to be the exception to the rule. I recognised one of his goons through the open driver's side window of a black Pajero and walked over to it. It seemed everyone in Manila with bucks had a penchant for a black Pajero. Well, at least it appeared that way.

"Tito, where's Ringo?" I asked.

"Get in. I'll take you to him," he said, gruffly.

I climbed into the passenger seat, mindful of my gun, ready in case it was another setup. Two henchmen were perched on the back seat like a pair of gargoyles.

"Where are we going?" I asked Tito, whom I had last met in my hotel room.

"One of the boss's clubs in Burgos Street."

Ah, the infamous P. Burgos Street—wall-to-wall girlie bars—the red-light district of Makati. I'd not been there, but I'd read about it.

CHAPTER EIGHT

WHEN YOU VISIT a city, if you're a bloke, you quickly learn about the red-light district by default, I guess. It was no surprise to learn Ringo was a stakeholder in the local sex industry.

Tito pulled the Pajero up outside a two-story white painted building with a flashing neon sign that read: Foxy's. I climbed out. A large overweight doorman opened the door to the club and while Tito parked the Pajero, the two gargoyles led me inside.

The music was pumping loud, and the lighting seductive. The gargoyles pointed upstairs, so I headed up the narrow dimly lit staircase. A couple of scantily dressed girls were on their way down and giggled past me. I must admit, the scallywag came out in me, and I purposely faced them so that they had to squeeze past and brush my chest with their boobs.

An older woman in a black suit with long pants met me at the top of the stairs and introduced herself.

"Mr. Stone, I am Mimi, mama-san of Foxy's. Please follow me."

She led me past a sushi bar and into a private room. I was immediately struck by the view through the floor-to-ceiling windows of the stage below, upon which half a dozen girls were slow dancing. I was impressed.

A single ceiling light flashed on at the back of me, and I turned to find Ringo seated under it in an armchair looking like an Emperor.

"Axis, glad you could make it... welcome to my club. Please sit down, make yourself comfortable."

Mimi closed the door behind her, and I flopped into a big comfy black leather armchair that was against the wall to the side of Ringo.

"What do you drink? You probably need one after your run-in with Arnel Gutierrez this afternoon."

"Is there anything you don't know, Ringo?"

"Yeah, who's got my girl!"

His eyes had an icy deadpan look that I didn't trust.

"Wish I could answer that for you, but so far my money's on Gutierrez. A Harvey Wallbanger, stirred not shaken, no vegetation."

Ringo pressed a button on the arm of his chair, and the door opened to Mimi.

"A bald Wallbanger for Mr Stone and the usual for me."

With the drinks ordered, he turned his attention back to Gutierrez.

"Why do you suspect him?"

"Avarice, that's enough to motivate any gold-digger," I said soberly.

"I don't know if he's got the guts or the brains to pull off something like that."

"So, you know him then?" I probed.

"Yeah, he was hanging around the Gramercy like a bad smell. I had to move him on."

I carefully changed the subject. "So, why bring me here and not to the Gramercy?"

"To show you how the other half lives."

"Didn't realize we were so divided. Besides, I've already had a brief encounter with the other half at the Star Bar?"

"Ha," he chuckled. "Rita Gutierrez, funny."

"Yeah, AKA Zorro... so why the tortured metaphor, what's funny?"

"Seems you've got problems with the entire Gutierrez family, Axis. Better ask your buddy Vargas how to deal with them. He's had plenty of experience."

"So I've heard."

"Was Cortez pleased with me bailing you out?"

"Yeah, like a hole in the head... I was thinking you only did it just to piss him off."

"Maybe, but let me get one thing straight with you, Stone. The law can be crooked here—business gets done by extortion—it's a way of life, a hangover, a psychologist would say, from our rebellious colonial days."

"Seems that's a common legacy of former Spanish colonies such as Mexico and most of Central and South America."

"That's what you get when there's little separation between Church and State," he said assertively.

"You can hardly complain; it makes for good business for a bloke like you... a joint like this couldn't exist in my country. I guess once you've got power and some money, you can stand over most anyone, and when you can't... you just buy them."

"You're a fast learner, Stone."

"I'd like to think so," I said cynically.

Our drinks arrived, and two things impressed me—first, my Wallbanger was dressed up as it should be, and two, the bird serving them was to die for. Ringo caught me gawking at her exquisite body.

"Tina, sit with Mr Stone," he commanded.

She sat beside me, and that immediately put the brakes on our conversation. A petite girl with lovely breasts and an hourglass figure, fluttering her eyelashes at me totally did my head in.

"What do you want to know, Ringo?" I asked.

"Newspapers say there's been a ransom demand. Has someone spoken to the kidnapper?"

"Yeah, he wants two million US in crypto, and that's thrown a different light on the case."

"I would have thought it throws a bad light on Gutierrez and Nelson."

"Isn't your money on Vargas?" I questioned.

"He doesn't need the money," he almost sang in a forced growl. He stood. "Downstairs," he snapped.

I followed him downstairs to the bar. The music was loud.

"You've got some nice ladies working here," I said loud enough to get above the beat.

"I turned an obsession into an industry," he said smugly.

He led to a dark alcove to talk in private.

"Want something to eat? We've got some nice Filipino appetizers, or there's sushi?"

"No thanks, already tried Bagoong and Balut, and I can't say I'll be backing up for seconds."

That got a snide chuckle out of him. We sat in the darkness, and I looked around. There were guys with bargirls secreted away in a dozen or so little curtained alcoves around the perimeter of the room, and a cavalcade of waitresses serving them. I had a good view of the stage, which was elevated four feet off the floor. On it, eight scantily clad girls line-danced real slow, to save energy, I guessed. The music tempo was such that it should've had them leaping about all over the shop. The half-dozen tables directly in front of the stage and along the small catwalk were packed with punters. All of the customers were Caucasian, except for a group of four Japanese or Koreans in suits. They had the most girls hanging off them and were carrying on like big spenders. I guess with the sort of company expense accounts they had, they were high-rollers, compared to the others at any rate.

I asked Ringo, "How does it work then?"

"What, the bar game?"

"Yeah."

"The girls make their money from the drinks customers buy them."

"How can they do that without getting plastered?"

"Their drinks are only shot glasses of orange juice... they cost the punter six bucks a pop, split fifty-fifty between the house and the girl. It's all on a tab that gets reckoned up after the customer pays his bill."

I grinned. "A license to print money."

The look on Raye's face had turned dead serious. "What's the scoop on the ransom? Does that mean Cortez will lay off my butt for a while?"

"Your nemesis—maybe so. Look, I'll tell you... when the Lovejoys spoke to Kitty, they heard lapping water and seabirds in the background. What does that say to you?"

"She's on a boat somewhere. What is this, a quiz?" he said soberly.

"Out of the suspects, who has a boat?"

"I do. Vargas. I don't know about Nelson, but he and Gutierrez would probably know someone who does."

"Where's your boat?" I asked.

"Subic Bay Yacht Club."

"And Vargas?"

"Manila Yacht Club, I'd say. So?"

"First, I need to search each of the suspects' boats, including yours. At the same time, find out if there are others."

I still wasn't sold on Ringo. There were only two possibilities for him buttering me up and playing the good guy—either he's head-over-heels for Kitty and wants her back, or he's the kidnapper.

Mimi popped out of the darkness behind us and whispered in Ringo's ear. It gave me a moment to study him. An honest-to-goodness rough diamond. I'd say born in poverty and self-made by brute force. He looked like the type that was a bully at school and a gang leader in his teens. Obviously loves his bling, drips in it as a badge of his success for all to see—from my experience, most gangsters are that way inclined. His steely eyes and hard-set jaw pair up with his ice-cold demeanour. His razor-sharp shrewdness evident in those eyes. But the one conspicuous trait that exuded from him like a force field was a brooding, uninhibited, deep violence. This guy was cruel, unrelenting, and I'd say with absolutely no sense of or understanding of guilt. Mimi left, and I continued.

"I don't get it," I mused.

"You don't get what?" he responded angrily.

"You've got enough muscle to find the kidnapper, why are you relying on me?"

"Thought that was obvious—I don't have a pipeline to the kidnapper. Whoever he is, he knows what I'm capable of. No, this has been carefully planned. This guy is smart, he's managed to cut me and the cops out of it by directly contacting the Lovejoys."

He had a valid point.

"All right," I said, standing to leave. "I need some shut-eye."

"One last question—who killed Chiki Dee?"

"If you're asking if I did, then set you up just to bust you out of jail—then no. You've got to remember you're a foreigner—word gets out on your movements—makes you an easy mark. Whoever killed Dee wanted to shut her up."

"I'll get onto Vargas' boat."

"What about Nelson and Gutierrez?" he asked.

"I'll get my associate Ricky to check into them."

"Ricky?"

"Ricky Esposo."

"He's an ex-cop. I know of him. Tell him to watch his back."

He signalled for Tito to take me home.

On the way to the Shang, I thought to myself, here I am, I've only been in Manila five minutes, and I'm rubbing shoulders with the biggest crook in town, getting chauffeur-driven, and my best mate is a millionaire. I love this gig.

I had just opened the door to my hotel room while checking my phone when I found a text message from Ricky I had missed. He had news on Gutierrez and wanted me to call him ASAP. I sat on the edge of the bed and dialled him.

"Ricky, hey, sorry it's late, there was too much noise at the club, I didn't hear my phone ring. He owns a bar on Burgos Street called

Foxy's... Yes, it was certainly an experience. So, what's the news? You're kidding me! Okay, meet me poolside at 9 A.M."

I hit the sack.

CHAPTER NINE

IT **WAS A** day with identical weather to yesterday. I was sipping my second coffee by the pool, taking in the view, and waiting for Ricky when he arrived.

"Hey, morning, boss," Ricky greeted.

"Ricky, I just drank the coffee I ordered for you," I replied.

"Sorry I'm late... traffic," he apologized.

I signalled a waiter for another coffee.

"So, our boy has a history, huh?" I said.

"More than that," Ricky said, pulling up a chair. "Arnel Gutierrez was arrested at the bust where Cortez's brother was murdered."

"Cortez's brother? That's quite a coincidence, isn't it? By the way, check out the woman getting into the pool," I commented.

"Focus, boss... And just like you, Arnel Gutierrez was held for only a few hours and then released without any charges," Ricky said.

"Hmm, sounds familiar... Anything else?" I asked, diverting my attention from the woman.

I couldn't take my eyes off the beautiful, buxom brunette posing at the edge of the pool. However, my attention was interrupted when her partner arrived, putting an end to my fantasy.

"After that, he tried his hand at business and went broke. You'll never guess who his investors were," Ricky continued.

"You've got me there," I admitted, finally paying attention.

She was looking my way, and our eyes locked.

"Bugs Bunny and Daffy Duck," Ricky snarled.

"Seriously?" I replied, vaguely.

Ricky got up from his chair.

"Maybe I'll come back when your logical head takes control over your lustful head, boss," he remarked.

That snapped me out of my carnal haze.

"I'm sorry, Ricky... Please, sit down... I don't know what's the matter with me... this town makes me uncontrollably aroused," I apologized. "Where were we?"

"You were going to guess the identity of the two investors with Arnel Gutierrez," Ricky said, sitting back down.

"I have no idea," I admitted, refocusing.

"Nick Vargas and Raymundo Gutierrez," Ricky revealed.

"Vargas! Raymundo, is that his father?" I asked.

"Yes."

"Well, I'll be damned. Did he also go broke?" I inquired.

"You bet he did, big time."

"What kind of business was it?" I inquired further.

"A bar."

"Why am I not surprised? Next, you'll be telling me it was the Star Bar. When did all this happen?" I questioned.

"Six months ago."

"How convenient," I remarked.

The bankruptcy provided a motive to support my suspicion of the Gutierrez family as the kidnappers. However, we needed more compelling evidence before presenting it to Cortez. Besides, I found the connection between Gutierrez and Cortez dubious and disturbing, to say the least.

"To recap, the Lovejoys said they heard birds and lapping water in the background when they spoke to Kitty... chances are she's being held on a boat. Raye mentioned that Vargas has a boat moored at the Manila Yacht Club. We need to check it out. We also need to find out if Nelson and the Gutierrez family own boats or have friends with boats, and if they do, where they're moored," I outlined our plan.

"I think Raye has a boat," Ricky added.

"Yes, he mentioned it, in a place called Subic Bay. We'll check that out as well," I agreed.

"We can't just board boats without permission, boss. They have armed guards," Ricky pointed out.

"Yeah, you're right. Let me worry about that. You focus on finding out the other information," I instructed.

While Ricky made phone calls, I took a quick dip in the pool to get a closer look at the brunette. The swim was refreshing, but the closer I got to her, the more I realized her looks weren't as appealing. By the time I was near her, I realized she was old enough to be my mother.

When I returned to Ricky, he already had some results.

"Boss, Nick Vargas sailed for Puerto Galera yesterday. Nelson owns a share in a boat. No news on Gutierrez yet," Ricky informed me.

"Puerto Galera? Where's that?" I asked, towelling myself down.

"It's an island down south near Batangas," he replied.

"I see. And where's Nelson's boat moored?" I inquired further.

"Subic Bay Yacht Club... same as Raye," Ricky answered.

"How far is that?" I questioned.

"It's a two-hour drive to the north," he replied.

"Let's do it," I decided.

Ricky made a call ahead and used his considerable influence to secure two rooms for us at the Subic Bay Yacht Club.

~ ~ ~

I enjoyed the drive to Subic Bay as it gave me a chance to see the countryside. It was fascinating to witness Mount Pinatubo looming in the distance as we entered Olongapo. I remembered the devastating footage of the volcano erupting in 1991 and the resulting destruction.

"It says on this map that's Mount Pinatubo," I remarked.

"Yes, boss, that's right. Did you know there's a conspiracy theory that the Americans dropped a small bomb in the volcano to trigger the eruption?" Ricky shared.

"You've got to be kidding. Why would they do that?" I asked, surprised.

"Because they needed an excuse to move the military bases out of Subic Bay and Clarke Airbase. Maintaining those bases was costing the US government a fortune, and they were considered outdated," Ricky explained.

"Why not just announce it then?" I questioned further.

"There were too many Filipino jobs dependent on the bases, and the government here wanted to keep the US military protection and the substantial lease payments they made each year for the massive complex," Ricky clarified.

"Well, I guess that makes sense. But to cause such a devastating eruption... Is there any proof?" I inquired.

"Seismologists had been monitoring the mountain, and there were no signs of an imminent eruption. It had been dormant for four hundred years. The native Aeta people living on the mountain also stated that the birds and animals hadn't shown any worrying signs, which are usually the first indication of an eruption. Then, they heard an explosion inside the mountain the day before the eruption. According to seismologists, they could distinguish between a natural explosion and a man-made one on their monitoring equipment. They claim the first explosion was definitely man-made. Another fact is that both the naval base and the airbase had everything packed up and ready to evacuate before the eruption," Ricky explained.

"Wow, that's mind-boggling," I commented.

The scenery dramatically changed as we crossed over the mountains and reached Subic Bay. Before us sprawled a picturesque town lining the coastline of the impressive azure blue bay, resembling delicate lace lingerie.

The yacht club offered a magnificent view of the marina and the bay. Ricky parked the car in the underground car park. It was a refreshing change to be in a tropical resort, away from the concrete jungle of Makati.

Since it was lunchtime, we decided to eat at the Cambusa Bistro within the club. We chose a window seat, attempting to identify which boat at the marina belonged to Raye and Nelson. After a satisfying meal, we checked into our respective rooms.

I settled into a comfy armchair with the intention of reading the newspaper when a knock on my door interrupted me. I reluctantly got up and opened the door.

"Sorry to disturb you, boss, but I got some information about Gutierrez," Ricky said.

"Come in, Ricky. Please, sit down and fill me in," I invited him inside.

"Gutierrez has a share in a boat that's up for sale. It's also here at the marina," Ricky informed me.

"We're in luck then," I remarked.

"It's cheaper to moor a boat here than at the Manila Yacht Club," Ricky suggested.

"Go downstairs and check the guest register, see if any familiar names have shown up in the last month. Also, check the marina security. I can't see any guards from here," I instructed him.

"Okay, will do, boss," Ricky acknowledged.

"I'll wait here," I replied.

While he was gone, I studied the marina's layout from my window. Three wharves extended into Subic Bay like withered fingers. All the moored boats were clearly visible from the yacht club, presenting a challenge for our unauthorized boarding plan.

After a while, Ricky called me from downstairs and suggested we have a drink by the pool. I gladly accepted and made my way down.

~ ~ ~

As I stepped out of the elevator, I immediately spied an attractive woman at the reception. From behind, she looked incredibly appealing. I lingered, trying to catch a glimpse of her face. Suddenly, she turned around, and I quickly ducked for cover when I recognised Bianca Gutierrez. Assuming Arnel might be nearby, I swiftly scanned the lobby but saw no sign of him. Why would she be here alone, especially after yesterday's incident at Café Havana?

I slipped into the corridor leading to the pool. Ricky had a Wallbanger waiting for me, desperately in need of a haircut. What is it with Yacht Clubs and overgrown vegetation?

"Guess who I just saw checking in?" I couldn't help but share with Ricky.

"Who, boss?" he asked.

"Bianca Gutierrez," I revealed.

"Well, you won't believe this, boss, but all of them—Raye, Nelson, and Arnel Gutierrez—have been here in the last four weeks, but only once," Ricky disclosed.

"That makes Nelson a liar. He claimed he hasn't been here in months. I don't know about you, Ricky, but this case keeps getting crazier by the minute. Do we know which boat belongs to whom?" I asked.

"Sure do, boss."

"Are there any guards?" I inquired.

"No security, but sometimes owners post guards on board," Ricky answered.

"Phew, it's hot here," I complained.

We were too exposed by the pool, making it necessary to be less conspicuous with Bianca and possibly her brother nearby. We finished our drinks and agreed to have dinner in our rooms, meeting up at midnight in a dark alcove we had identified near the marina entrance. From there, we would embark on a covert mission to search each of the boats.

Ricky got off the elevator on his floor, and I continued to the upper deck. On my way to my room, a door opened in the corridor, and Bianca stepped out. There was no avoiding her.

"Bee! Small world! Fancy seeing you here," I greeted her smoothly.

"I've got nothing to say to you, Stone," she snapped.

"I may not have much to say, but you certainly have a lot on display. You're quite a sight," I commented.

"Save the cheesy compliments for someone else, Stone," she retorted.

She tried to walk away, but realising my cover was blown, I needed to prevent her from alerting Arnel. I blocked her path with an outstretched arm, then moved closer in a seductive manner, altering my tone to a bedroom whisper.

"Look, I know we got off on the wrong foot—" I began.

"Excuse me, but a girl's best friends are her legs. Bye," she interrupted.

She couldn't get past me.

"But all good friends have to part sometime," I said warmly, with a smile. "Let me make it up to you. How about finishing that glass of French champers in my room?"

I sensed her resolve weakening.

"I don't feel dressed for cocktails," she hesitated.

"No need to change on my account. I like you just the way you are," I assured her.

Her eyes flashed, and she appreciated my Billy Joel reference.

We slipped into my room, and she settled on the couch while I fetched a half bottle of Veuve Clicquot from the minibar.

"It's odd, both of us being here," I mentioned, popping the cork and pouring two glasses.

"I know why I'm here. How about you?" she purred, raising an eyebrow inquisitively.

"I'm a member of the Royal Sydney Yacht Club," I lied. "They offered me a night here, and with it being the weekend..."

I handed her a glass, and we clinked them together.

"Ah, I see," she said doubtfully. "You're here alone?"

Again, I had to lie. It seemed to become a habit with her.

"Yes, and you?" I asked, sitting at one end of the three-seater couch, creating distance between us.

"Sometimes I come here on weekends when I need to escape Makati. We have a boat at the marina," she revealed.

"Alone?" I inquired.

"Hmm, sometimes I bring someone to keep me company... but not this time," she hinted.

"Hmm," I echoed.

Before I realised it, she had placed her glass down and slid along the couch until she was right next to me. I could feel the warmth of her thigh gently pressing against mine. Her lips were tantalisingly close, her fragrance intoxicating.

"Well," she said sleepily. "What are you waiting for? Here I am, in your room, with soft lights and a mood that sends shivers down my spine, and a drink that notoriously unleashes my primal desires. Are you a man or a mouse? Or did you just want to ask me questions? Have I misjudged you?"

Her invitation was too enticing to resist or even consider refusing. I mean, what was I supposed to do when she made her intentions so obvious? I set down my glass.

Our lips met, starting gently and then growing more passionate as our desires took over.

CHAPTER TEN

I **WOKE WITH** a jolt and checked the time: it was 12:17 A.M., well past the midnight rendezvous with Ricky. I dressed in a panicked frenzy, careful not to wake the sleeping beauty.

There was only one staff member at the reception, the lobby otherwise void of life. I slipped past him effortlessly, and out through the large glass doors that opened onto the marina. Thirty or so boats were moored there, only two of which were illuminated by cabin lights. That suggested the rest were likely unoccupied. I arrived at the dark alcove, our designated meeting point, but Ricky was nowhere to be found. Then, in the shadows, I spotted a body lying face down on the ground. It had to be Ricky. I turned him over to find the aftermath of a brutal beating. Blood dripped from the back of his head, forming a pool on the ground that shimmered under the moonlight. I felt for a pulse - it was there. Relief washed over me; he was alive, but barely. His pulse was weak. Realising I needed an ambulance immediately, I rushed back to enlist the help of the lone receptionist.

I accompanied Ricky in the back of the ambulance to the Subic Medical Center, then endured an agonising wait while an emergency team worked on him. Eventually, a nurse emerged from the ER and informed me they'd stabilized him, suggesting there was no point in my staying and to return later. Guilt consumed me. I'd failed my friend, the same one who'd saved my life only nights before. The little head had once again overruled the big one, and this wasn't the first time.

I chose to walk back to the Yacht Club to mull over the events, but the guilt trailed behind me. Kicking stones, I pondered who could have attacked Ricky; perhaps Arnel? Who else knew our plans? Had he been mugged? The answers would have to wait until Ricky regained consciousness.

~ ~ ~

Upon returning to my room, I discovered Bee had flown the coup. It was understandable. She probably woke up, found me missing, and retreated to her own room. The sun was up, and sleep was far from my mind, so I decided to go for a buffet breakfast at the Club café. On my way, I knocked on Bianca's door, but there was no response. I assumed she was still sleeping.

As I exited the elevator, my phone, nicknamed "The Terrible Tango," blared into life. I answered; it was Cortez.

"Hey Sancho, news travels fast. I didn't inform you about my coming here because... Right, you're taking the helicopter... Okay... I'll see you there in three hours."

He was angry, and rightfully so. I'd taken matters into my own hands again, and this time someone got seriously injured. I'd have to face the music.

I was gazing out the café window at the marina when The Terrible Tango rang again. This time, it was the hospital notifying me that Ricky was out of danger and awake. It was a piece of good news.

~ ~ ~

By the time I reached the hospital room, Ricky already had visitors: Cortez and two uniformed Subic Barangay police officers. At Cortez's nod, the officers vacated the room. Ricky was a sorry sight. His face was a pale, battered, and bruised canvas, with one eye swollen shut. His right hand was bandaged, with his fingers set in splints.

"Hey Ricky, glad to see you're still with us. Has Cortez been grilling you?" I asked.

Speaking was obviously a struggle for him, but he managed a response. "There were two of them, boss," he groaned. "No faces... balaclavas... tire irons. One held my hand while the other smashed my fingers." He winced in pain as he held up his injured right hand.

I winced in sympathy. It looked excruciating. "Did they say anything?" I asked.

"Only my name. They called it out and attacked from behind."

This detail meant they knew exactly who he was, which ruled out a random mugging. A nurse entered the room then, demanding that we leave. But Cortez had one final question.

"Ricky, who else knew you were going to search the boats?"

The question clearly troubled Ricky; he didn't want to disclose his contact at police HQ.

I stepped in. "Ricky, whoever you told likely set you up."

"Where were you, boss?"

"You'll have to leave now!" The nurse insisted.

"I was with Bianca Gutierrez," I admitted guiltily, avoiding eye contact.

"Maybe she set us up," Ricky suggested through gritted teeth, the pain becoming more evident.

The implication of his words hit me like a punch to the gut.

"My contact at HQ is Vic Cruz," Ricky finally confessed.

Upon hearing the name Vic Cruz, Cortez's demeanour changed noticeably. He abruptly turned and marched out of the room without uttering a word.

"Get some rest, Ricky," I told him before chasing after Cortez.

"Sancho! Wait!"

He halted outside the hospital, sparking up a cigarette.

"What's the matter? It was Vic Cruz's name, wasn't it?" I asked.

The cigarette seemed to calm him down somewhat.

"There's a Starbucks a couple of blocks away. We'll talk there," he replied, clearly irritated.

~ ~ ~

The officers gave us a lift to Starbucks, then waited outside for us. We ordered some coffees and found a seat.

"So, tell me about Vic Cruz?" I urged.

"It's a story I didn't think you needed to know, but it's now relevant. My brother, Pablo, was an operative for the Philippine National Police Anti-Illegal Drugs Group, which is headed by Vic Cruz."

"He's the head of the narcotics squad?"

"Yes. Pablo was undercover in a drug ring suspected of being run by Ringo Raye. His cover name was Tony Lamont. There was a significant Shabu deal happening, which Pablo had been infiltrating for a year."

"Shabu?"

"Crystal meth. It's called Shabu here. Pablo, along with a gang member, loaded a truck with a container hiding the drugs at the high-security enclosure of the Manila Container Terminal. He had informed his superior in the drug task force, who planned to ambush the truck at the exit gate. But, the task force assembled at the wrong gate due to someone ratting out Pablo. As the truck was leaving the terminal, Pablo was shot. The truck careened into traffic, crashed, and exploded. The passenger who shot him managed to escape before the explosion, but Pablo wasn't so lucky."

"I'm sorry for your loss... Were the drugs destroyed?"

"The truck was entirely burned. Forensics informed me that Pablo had been shot point-blank before the explosion."

"So where does Cruz fit in?" I asked.

"Cruz was the commanding officer. The operation was a collaborative effort between customs, the PDEA—Philippine Drug Enforcement Agency, and the police. Since then, I've been trying to prove Cruz's involvement but without success."

"So, you think he was part of it?"

"He had to be. Cruz sent them to the wrong gate, and he's the only one who could've blown Pablo's cover."

"There was no police investigation?"

"Cruz is too influential and deeply connected with the underworld, senators... anyone of note, really. He has dirt on all of them."

"How is he able to do that?"

"Cruz operates by his own rules, accountable to no one. For instance, when Pablo was first recruited into the drug squad under Cruz's direct command, Cruz eventually confided in him—possibly bragging—that he once needed a court decision to swing in his favour. To achieve this, he planted drugs on the presiding judge's eldest son and then had him arrested. Naturally, the decision went his way."

"So, you're saying Pablo knew about Cruz's deeds?"

"Yes, Pablo had collected enough evidence on Cruz to bring him down. But Cruz's task force was created directly by the President."

"Was Pablo planning to expose him?"

"It's plausible."

"Were you working with Pablo to that end?"

"Let's just say we had a shared interest."

"So, there was no inquiry into the botched drug bust?"

"Cruz swept it under the rug. If I were to accuse him of anything, I'd end up in Manila Bay with concrete shoes."

So, you went after Raye?'

"Yes, I saved some of Pablo's files before Cruz could destroy them. They pointed the finger at Raye behind the deal without spelling out his name. But I figured if I could get Raye I could ultimately get Cruz."

"Raye must have lost a fortune in that fire?"

"They both did ... it was one of the biggest drug hauls ever in this country."

"Didn't Pablo tell anybody the name of his passenger?"

"Only Cruz would have known, which further implicates him … he of course denied it. Later, my task force arrested Arnel Gutierrez on suspicion of conspiracy to murder from a tip-off, but Cruz had him released within hours without charge or my knowledge."

"That's suspicious." It confirmed the story Ricky had given me.

"There is more, the Vargas family owns and operates the high security container depot where the drugs arrived, and Bianca Gutierrez was the girlfriend of Nick Vargas at the time."

"Damn! This is all somehow connected to the kidnapping isn't it?" I said, astounded.

We were at last getting somewhere, and Ringo was beginning to look decidedly ugly.

"I still want to search the boats," I told him anxiously.

"Who owns them?"

I pulled my phone. "Ricky texted me the info … wait, right … Ringo owns Bodyshot, Nelson has Go See and the Gutierrez family has Sarap. Can we get a search warrant?"

"No, can't help you there it's maritime services jurisdiction. I am due back at HQ in an hour. I would be dropping that line of investigation if I were you Stone, seeing your intentions seem to be too well known."

"Yeah, I think you might be right."

"They will release Ricky this afternoon. Best collect him and you two hightail it back to Makati quick smart."

"I hear yer."

~ ~ ~

The uniforms dropped me back at the Subic Yacht Club, and then took Cortez to the police helipad.

I went directly to Bianca's room. I needed to know if she'd set me up. After bashing on the door for five minutes, I quit and went down to reception to ask if she'd checked out. I got an affirmative. Angry with myself, I went to the swimming pool, ordered a drink, and, staring mindlessly into space, noticed Sancho's police chopper flashing across the cerulean sky bound for Makati. That brought me back to reality and I focused my attention on the marina. I decided to take a stroll for a sly gander at the boats.

The blazing hot sun and the humidity had my armpits leaking like a faucet with a busted washer. There was little activity to be seen on the wharves. By its proximity to the amenities, the first wharf obviously catered to deluxe boats—they were bigger than all the others. The next wharf accommodated the middle-class moorings, and then the economy wharf. Figuring Raye thought highly of himself, I decided to check the deluxe wharf for his boat, Bodyshot. I tried to look as inconspicuous as my western frame would permit and strolled out along the wharf with my hands clasped behind my back like Prince Philip, stopping and acting to peer into the green water for fish. I'd made it halfway along when I sighted two unfriendly-looking guards eyeballing me from a boat deck. I nonchalantly retreated and then continued along the middle-class wharf and quickly came upon a Halvorsen Broadwater 32 with the name Sarap emblazoned on its stern. It was the boat the Gutierrez family used in syndicate with partners. I knelt down and messed with my shoelace while surreptitiously taking in the topography for a return visit later after dark. There didn't seem to be anyone aboard, so I carried on. At the end of the wharf, I found a Rhodes 27 sailing boat named Go See, again with no one on board. It was Nelson's style all right: a battered old clunker with its hull coated in barnacles.

~ ~ ~

I'd only just entered the room when the phone rang. It was the hospital: Ricky was ready to be discharged.

Just on dusk, the uniforms dropped Ricky at the Yacht Club, and I helped him up to my room. He could walk, but only gingerly.

"We'll leave later tonight, mate. I'll drive. But first, I'm going to search the boats like we planned," I told him firmly.

"Don't be crazy, boss. It isn't safe on your own!"

"Let me worry about that, mate. I've extended the checkout time, so just kick back and chill. I'll be back soon."

The sun had gone down, and the lobby was deserted when I crossed it to slip out through the doors onto the marina. I made it undetected. But Ricky was right... the atmosphere was thick with the stench of danger.

I walked quickly onto the wharf... there was no one around, just a boat tying up at the end of the closest one: the deluxe wharf.

When I climbed aboard Sarap, I found the cabin door open, so I crept inside. It took only minutes to determine that there was nothing to be found. Next was Nelson's boat, Go See. A yacht is much more difficult to board because it's far less sturdy than a cruiser. The damn thing rocked and rolled, and I stumbled about in the dark like a blind man on a trampoline. I nearly ended up on my butt trying to step down from the deck onto the companionway. When I reached for the door handle to the cabin, it flew open on its own, and a big burly dude all in black dived out and tackled me around the hips. We hit the deck together with a massive thump. Built like a tank, he was getting the better of me until I managed to lift my knee into his groin. He immediately doubled up in pain. I took the opportunity to escape. As I jumped onto the gunwale, he reached up from the deck, grabbed my trouser leg, and lifted himself enough to land a massive kidney punch. I went down gasping for air. Standing over me, he let fly with a barrage of punches to my face. I felt a stream of warm blood running down my cheek... he'd split my eyebrow—another bloody scar! All I could think of was, how am I going to get out of this?

CHAPTER ELEVEN

THE ANSWER CAME from just above me in the form of the boom. I mustered all my strength, deflected a vicious left hook from him with my forearm, struggled to my feet, grabbed the boom, and swung it at him as hard as I could. It caught him by surprise as he was getting to his feet and smacked him right across the bridge of the nose, knocking him backwards base over apex. Proud of my work, I looked down at him sprawled out on the deck. He was out cold and urgently in need of rhinoplasty. I grabbed his shirt front and snarled, "Hey, you!" There was no response, so I slapped him one across the cheek. "Who's your boss?" He came to and grumbled something in Tagalog. It was no use. Feeling pretty shabby after the beating, I gave up on him and made a quick exit as fast as my wobbly legs could carry me back to the sanctuary of the Yacht Club.

~ ~ ~

We were packed and on the Luzon Highway, driving south for Makati faster than you could say 'Jack Robinson'. There was no way I was going to hang around the Yacht Club to risk another beating — I preferred my face the way it was before the Go See brawl.

My mind was echoing with the thought of why I'd been attacked on Go See. Did I need to promote Nelson to number one on my hit list of suspects? I was kicking myself for not getting the chance to locate and check out Raye's boat, Bodyshot.

Ricky was asleep when we got to Balintawak: the off-ramp from the freeway to Epifanio de los Santos, or EDSA Avenue, as it's known locally. I was just managing to cope with driving on the other side of the road when I suddenly found myself under siege from chaotic traffic. The lack of street signage and the confusion made me panic. "Hey, Ricky! Wake up, pal! There are roads going everywhere, which one do I take?"

He opened one badly bruised eye, yawned, and then mumbled, "Turn right on EDSA, that's the big street, boss, it will take us all the way to Makati." Then he promptly fell back asleep.

~ ~ ~

I pulled the car into the Dela Rosa Apartments on Ayala Avenue, Makati, and got the concierge to help Ricky up to his apartment. I thought it best to leave his car in the apartment car park and then walk to the Shang. By the time I reached it, the humidity had my armpits leaking like a sieve.

Sporting a cut eyebrow and a split lip, and looking like I'd lost a prize fight, I tried to slip through the reception area to the elevator without being noticed. As soon as I got into my room, I dived into a steaming hot shower.

After cleaning up my wounds, it was time to ring Lola Lovejoy for a progress report. Her warm, sultry voice answered. "Hello."

"Lola, hi … its Axis."

"I've been worried about you, it's been—"

"I'm fine, I'm fine," I cut her off. "Ricky, my off-sider, and I took a bit of a beating, but we're okay. Have you heard anything?"

"I can't believe you just said that so casually! You took a beating? My lord! Why?"

"Oh, just an occupational hazard," I played it up big to get a little sympathy.

"Are you hurt?"

"Just a split lip and a few bruises. Ricky spent the night in hospital, has a few broken fingers but he'll live. So, have you heard anything from the kidnapper?"

"No, we haven't heard a thing … we're running out of time, aren't we?"

"We are, but I reckon he'll take us right down to the wire and call you tomorrow."

"Do you have any news to tell Dad? Anything, please, I don't want to just tell him you guys took a beating, it will only make him worry more."

"Tell him I've established a good working relationship with the cop in charge, Sancho Cortez, and that we've narrowed it down to three main suspects, but we need conclusive evidence before we can make a move on any of them."

"Oh Axis," she whimpered, "I don't know what I'd do without you."

"Just tell your dad things are progressing. Call me as soon as you hear something. Okay?"

She sighed, "Ah, thank you, Axis, and … good night." She threw me a kiss through the phone, and it landed like a left hook. The idea that Bianca had set me up was still nagging at me. I checked the phone numbers Ricky had given me, found hers and rang. When it answered it was Bianca but she quickly handed the phone over to someone else.

"Who's this?" A male voice demanded.

"Axis Stone, is that you, Arnel?"

"You've got the wrong number."

I knew it was him. "Hey, wait! I know it was you that hit Ricky at the Yacht Club. Do you know how I know? Because it was a cowardly attack and you're a coward. So, let me tell you what I'm going to do about that. I'm coming after you, and know this: I've got the skill set to mess you up. Now, you might argue you have the same. Well then, one way or another we're going to find out, aren't we, son?" I used the age and experience stand-over routine.

"Go to hell, Stone!" he growled, and hung up.

I expected that. At least I'd got it off my chest and issued a challenge. It felt good. Now, to deal with the next quandary. Why had I been attacked on Go See? The finger was firmly pointed at Nelson. I know he's doing it tough, but is that motive enough for him to kidnap Kitty? I checked his number and rang.

A female answered. "Hello."

"Hi, I want to speak with Buddy Nelson. Tell him it's private investigator Axis Stone."

She went to get him, and I could hear him in the background berating her for not hanging up on me.

"What do you want, Stone?" The voice at the other end growled.

"We need to talk, Nelson," I snapped back.

"I've got nothing more to say to you."

"Unless you want to get busted for aiding and abetting a kidnapping, I suggest we talk, and real soon."

There was a pregnant pause while he considered his options. I knew he didn't have any.

"All right, all right, Stone, have it your way. Hop a cab to my apartment. I'll text you the address."

This time I packed my piece, unwilling to take any chances with the bum.

~ ~ ~

The cabby found Colonnade Residences on Legazpi Street. It was stupid taking a cab; I could see the Shang three blocks away. Cursing, I went inside. It was an old-style, Spanish-looking block with a rickety old elevator servicing the nine floors. A fake Roman plaque finished in gold leaf gilt identified the door to Nelson's suite, number 66. I knocked loudly and then waited. After what seemed like days, the door opened just enough for me to spy a pair of ice-blue eyes staring coldly at me.

"What the hell do you want?" The voice belonging to the eyes asked. I pushed the door open wider — her red hair was long and spread in wild profusion around her shoulders. She was wearing a thin crimson silk robe, belted around her waist... the hem reached the middle of her thighs. She was exotic-looking, maybe Russian.

"The name's Stone. I'm here to meet Buddy Nelson."

"He's not here," she snapped arrogantly with a heavy Eastern European accent. She tried to close the door in my face, but I jammed it with my foot.

"Hey, I haven't finished talking to you. When will Nelson be back?" I growled.

"No idea." The arctic tone of her voice didn't go at all with the Manila humidity. I saw no point trying to talk logic with her; that would be about as stupid as trying to catch a cab on a rainy day.

"Is there a problem, Zelda?" A male voice resounded from somewhere behind her.

"A dude called Stone," she grunted. "Wants to talk with Buddy, he sez."

The male voice thundered, "I'll take care of it!"

"I'd be glad if you did," she called out, frigidly. "The way he's staring at me now, I figure wearing a robe is a complete waste of time."

She turned away, and her place was taken by the owner of the male voice: a young Filipino hunk in his mid-twenties with unruly black hair and built like a Sherman tank... obviously a bodybuilder.

"I'm Al Perez," he said. "You are?"

"Stone, Private investigator. Are you hard of hearing?"

His upper lip rose up into a snarl. "So?"

"I spoke with Buddy on the phone, he invited me here."

"Fascinating!" he yawned carefully. "Your client wouldn't be Nick Vargas, would it?"

"My client's identity is confidential. Can I come in?"

"No way," he said curtly. "Got any ID?"

I sighed annoyed, pulled out my wallet, and flashed my license. He wasn't impressed.

"Goodbye Stone," he growled.

My foot was still in the doorjamb, so he couldn't slam it shut.

"Out!" he yelled and grabbed my shoulder. "You just ran out of time, Stone!"

I was wearing boots, so I kicked him hard in the shin. He let out a yelp and hopped about on one foot with both hands clasping the wound. I chopped the edge of my hand down across the side of his neck real hard. He hit the floor flat-out and stayed there.

The Russian woman came running right at me like a screaming banshee, her hands hooked into claws, her long nails driving toward my face. A tall, strong-looking girl around five-ten, it was ugly. Now, as a rule, I don't hit women, but this had to be an exception. I smacked her on the chin just hard enough to stop her in her tracks.

A voice rang out from behind me. "What are you doing to my actors, Stone?"

I swung around and found Nelson. "Just giving them some direction, they crossed the line," I assured him, smugly.

He pushed his big frame past me, stepped over the big hunk on the floor, and put a consoling arm around the Russian woman, who was holding her chin, teary-eyed.

"He hit me," she whimpered angrily.

"Self-defense," I countered.

"I can believe that... she can be a tigress, our Zelda. It's that Baltic blood," he mumbled, peering down at Perez sitting on the floor scratching his head, confused like someone had stolen his ice cream and he didn't know why. "Give him a hand into the bedroom, Zelda. I need to talk with Stone."

She put her hands on her hips and protested, "Why should I—?"

"Because I told you to, that's why... Okay?" he reprimanded loudly. "No arguments."

Pulling a scowling dark face, she helped Perez to his feet and then off to the bedroom.

Nelson sat down in his favourite armchair and motioned for me to sit in the two-seater opposite him. Impeccably dressed, around fifty and overweight, he stared at me with insolent disdain.

He asked in the kind of voice that strongly doubted it was possible, "What's this about, Stone?"

"I was at the Subic Bay Yacht Club earlier today and paid a visit to your boat, Go See. I got this in reward," I protested, pointing at my cut eyebrow.

"That's what you get for sticking your eyebrow into someone else's business." His voice gained added confidence from the slight wheedling tone I'd injected into my own, and a condescending smile spread across his lips. "Go See! Ha! The last time I was in Subic, I didn't even go see her myself."

"You were there only weeks ago. Are you asking me to believe you have nothing to do with the boat?"

"You're damn right I am... you never stop spending money on an old clunker like that piece of flotsam. Wanna buy it?"

"That's probably the worst sales pitch I've ever heard."

"You were looking for Kitty on my boat, weren't you? You could've just asked me if she was on it. Why would I want to kidnap her?"

"Money."

"Ha! What money?" he snapped.

"The kidnapper wants two million US in crypto."

"Hope he isn't holding his breath to get it."

"Now, why would you say that?" I asked cynically.

He reclined, crossed his big legs, and checked the fingernails on his pudgy hands like he didn't give a rat's. "Oh, a while ago I needed an investor for a big concert here and asked Kitty if her family would buy in. She laughed and admitted that after her mother died a few years back and her father—"

"Winston."

"Yeah, Winston, started playing the Gee Gees and got his fingers badly burnt."

The news rocked me back in my chair. It could explain Winston's ill health.

"So, he lost a few skins at the races. So what?"

"A few skins? Ha! Word is, he owes millions to Gold Coast bookies. He's so desperate, it's common knowledge he can be bought to fix trials."

"You're having me on!"

"Not likely... put it this way, Stone," he eyeballed me with a sarcastic grin on his ugly fat mush. "You better have got your fee up front." He laughed, and his jowls bounded up and down like jelly.

I snapped, "You saying he wouldn't be able to pay the ransom?"

"You got that part right, pal," he chuckled, finding it most amusing.

It was the last thing I wanted to hear. Nelson was far too slimy to be trusted. But he was now off my list of suspects. Kidnapping wasn't his style, but after what he told me, I now had serious doubts about Winston's solvency. I needed to ensure I wouldn't be the loser in this gig. If Nelson was right, then the Lovejoys weren't being straight with me, and that wasn't kosher.

CHAPTER TWELVE

I **HAD JUST** left Nelson's apartment block and was heading back to the Shangri-La when The Terrible Tango started playing. I answered the call. "Stone. Yeah, Ringo, I'm in Makati. Where are you? Twin Towers on Ayala Avenue, yeah, I know where that is... what's this about? Okay, I'll meet you there in fifteen." I estimated that's how long it would take me to walk from Legazpi Street to Twin Towers at midnight.

As I ambled along the sidewalk, I pondered what Ringo was up to. Was he merely using me to keep tabs on the investigation? Was he setting me up? A cunning fox with a motive, he undoubtedly had the means to orchestrate a kidnapping. Everything that occurred at Subic Bay could have been part of an elaborate scheme by him to throw me off the scent. Was he in collaboration with the crooked cop, Cruz? Why was Bianca at the Yacht Club? Why did she leave without saying a word? Were Ringo and the Gutierrez family involved in the kidnapping? I was convinced that spending a bit more time socializing with Ringo, at great risk to my person, could either yield answers to some of these nagging questions or land me a spot on a mortuary slab.

~ ~ ~

I walked into Ringo's upscale penthouse apartment. He wasn't alone; three women were lazily spread out on couches in various stages of undress, posing as if they were centrefolds in Penthouse magazine. "Having a party?" I asked, pegging the skin on show.

"Nothing out of the ordinary," he replied, smirking arrogantly. He made his way to a well-stocked bar. "How about a bodyshot, Stone. Ever had one?"

"Nope, but it sounds a smidgen dangerous."

"Oh, it is … but well worth the risk, I assure you." He gestured for one of the girls to move to a vacant three-seat sofa. "Our guest will have a bodyshot, Suzy."

She moved with a graceful ease and reclined on the sofa, posing vulnerably. Ringo approached her with a bottle of Russian Vodka. "Come, Stone, experience one of our Manila delights."

I joined him next to the supine girl. He filled a shot glass with vodka, lifted her dress just below her breasts, and then filled her navel with vodka.

"There, a bodyshot … drink, my friend."

I got the idea, leaned down, and sipped the warm liquid. It tasted surprisingly good. By the time I'd taken a body shot from the navel of each of the three women, twice, I was feeling pretty loaded. It was a heady experience.

Ringo, grinning widely, asked, "So, which girl tasted the best, Stone?"

"All of them."

Ringo dismissed the girls with a flick of his finger, waited for them to leave, and then his smirk hardened. "I heard your ex-cop buddy met with an accident."

"You mean Ricky? Yeah, he got mugged."

"You were in Subic?"

"Let's cut to the chase, Ringo, you know damn well I was and what I was looking for. What I want to know is … what's your game?"

"I don't play games, Stone, I invent them."

"We just played bodyshot, so I guess that either makes you a liar or a hypocrite."

The confrontation caused his eyes to narrow. "I didn't invent the bodyshot, Stone ... Those are tough words for someone who knows my reputation," he growled, rotating one of the many rings on his fingers, clearly irritated. "I made it clear to you, my only interest is in finding Kitty."

"What about your interest in Tony Lamont? And what about your connection with the Gutierrez family?"

He leaned back in the lounge chair, scrutinizing me through squinted eyes. "Questions like that could get you killed."

"An occupational hazard."

"Alright, I'll play along with your little game, Stone. I don't have anything to do with the Gutierrez family, if you'd done your homework, you'd know that they were partners at one time with Vargas. As for Tony Lamont ... never heard of him. Your serve."

"What about Bianca?"

"Before she got her gold-digging claws into Vargas, I had a roll between the sheets with her a few times. But for me, she's high maintenance."

"A few times ... from what I've heard you were a regular donor."

"As you can see, Stone," he gestured in the direction the women had gone. "I make regular donations."

I asked an even tougher question. "Are you partners with Vic Cruz?"

"I have a lot of partners, Stone."

"But this one's a cop, head of the Philippines National Police Anti-Illegal Drugs Group. Does that ring a bell, Ringo?"

"Do I look like the kind of guy that would have anything to do with narcs or any government agency? You're barking up the wrong tree, Stone."

"You've already shown your influence with the cops by getting me out of jail."

"Bribing the cops is a way of life here..."

I wasn't getting anywhere with him … he was far too clever to trip up with that line of questioning. Besides, I could sense his growing impatience.

"I need to check your boat," I stated firmly.

"For Kitty, ha! Be my guest … I'd be thrilled and surprised if you find her on it."

We sized each other up. Ringo had calmed down. I knew his type — even in a fistfight, he'd remain calm. Men like him were dangerous, unscrupulous, and void of fear or guilt. He reached into his jacket, causing me to flinch as I thought he was reaching for a gun. To my relief, he pulled out a Havana cigar and lit it. He blew a ring of smoke into the air and fixed his predatory gaze on me. "Do you think Nelson kidnapped her?"

"Unlikely, he doesn't have the entrance fee. Why would Vargas kidnap her? She's already his girl … and he doesn't need the ransom."

He puffed on his cigar, deep in thought. "Then it must be Cortez. There is no-one else."

"So, you think Cortez has the brains to set up a complicated transfer?"

"Sure, they investigate cop corruption here all the time."

I decided to dig a little deeper. "Do you know anything about Winston Lovejoy's gambling debts?"

"I've heard rumours."

"Would that put him in the mix?"

"I wouldn't rule it out. That's enough, time for some fun. You can use the guest room." He stood up, extinguished his cigar in the ashtray, and disappeared into his bedroom. His game wasn't for me. I left.

~ ~ ~

I took the elevator down twenty-five floors to the ground level and exited the building. As I walked through the early morning light, I realised that my conversation with Ringo hadn't brought me any closer to a solution; if anything, I was even more lost. The idea of Winston Lovejoy being involved was doing my head in.

Deciding to get some breakfast, I headed to the Pancake House in Greenbelt, the only place open at that hour and nearby. I was preparing myself for a long day. The ransom deadline was fast approaching and I was nowhere near finding Kitty. Ringo blamed Cortez; Nelson pointed at Winston Lovejoy; Cortez blamed Cruz; and I was focusing on the Gutierrez family. Meanwhile, Ricky was at home nursing his wounds. I felt a pang of anxiety, thinking that I might have seriously miscalculated by not taking the kidnapper's demands more seriously. I headed back to my hotel room to wait it out.

I fell asleep and was jolted awake at 11 A.M. by the ringtone of The Terrible Tango. It was Lola, and she sounded panicked.

"Axis ... oh my God, what are we going to do?" she cried.

"Lola ... you've obviously heard from him, calm down. What did he say?" I asked, rubbing the sleep from my eyes.

"We heard from him all right, and it wasn't very pleasant."

I wasn't sure what she had been expecting, but it was never going to be pleasant. "So, what did he say?" I urged, yawning and blinking my eyes to get my senses together. I've never been a morning person until I've had my first coffee.

"He said he would only deal with one person, so we gave him your cell number," she explained.

"Go on."

"He will text you the general location for the exchange. Once you confirm that you're there, he'll text you the exact location. Kitty will be there, in full view, but ..." she whimpered, "he said she will be rigged to an explosive device that he can detonate remotely!"

Her news was grim — no wonder she was panicked. "Tell me more," I said calmly. "Take a deep breath."

After a pause, she managed to collect herself. "He said we would have fifteen minutes to transfer the money. Only when he confirms receipt will he disarm the bomb," she started crying again. "What are we going to do, Axis? We don't have that kind of money."

"Sorry to be a realist, kid, but you really only have one option."

"You're not listening, Axis, we don't have the money."

"I hear you loud and clear Lola, but that doesn't change the situation. Here's a thought: why not contact Nick Vargas and ask him for a loan? He loves Kitty and he has the bread. I'll text you his number, but you need to act quickly."

"I don't know if Dad will agree to more debt, he's already—"

"The clock is ticking, Lola. Talk to Winston, make a decision, and call me back. I'll wait for your call ... and while you're at it, make sure my fee is covered."

"Okay, will do, thank you Axis, bye."

I ended the call, understanding now that Nelson had been right all along: the Lovejoys were drowning in debt. Now they had a tough decision to make: call the kidnapper's bluff or go deeper into debt. From my perspective, they didn't really have much of a choice.

CHAPTER THIRTEEN

AFTER I TEXTED Lola the number of Nick Vargas, I phoned Cortez. "Sancho, it's Axis Stone. We've had contact."

"Thank goodness."

"Yeah, it was looking grim for a while there. Anyway, they've made me the point person and I'll be getting exchange instructions via text."

"When?"

"I don't know, whenever he's ready, I guess."

"How do you want to play it?"

"Well, it doesn't sound like we'll have a lot of choices. He'll have Kitty wired to a bomb that can be remotely detonated. Once the money is in his account, he'll deactivate it."

"Do you believe he'd do that?"

"Not on your life, but we don't have much choice, do we?"

"I suppose you're right. Any more ideas on his identity?" he asked.

"No, nothing. How about you? Any word on Cruz?" I queried.

"He's been out of town for the last two weeks."

"That sounds suspiciously timely. But it doesn't fit in with Ricky talking to him."

"Unless Ricky calls his cellphone," Cortez suggested.

"Yeah, that makes sense. He could be our man. Look, if he is, he wouldn't be working alone. Chiki Dee said two guys bundled Kitty into a waiting car, that's three counting the driver."

"And two guys attacked Ricky in Subic," Cortez added.

"Exactly."

This guy Cruz was registering at a nine on the Richter scale.

"Better grill some of his colleagues," I suggested.

"That's easier said than done, amigo."

"Hate to say it, Sancho, but that's your job."

"Okay, okay, I get it. But what about the ransom? Do the Lovejoys have the money? Word is they are not doing well financially."

"Seems everyone knew about that except me. I've put Lola Lovejoy in touch with Vargas, maybe he'll kick the bin."

"It's a lot of money, even for someone like him. He won't be able to arrange it that quickly."

"I'm sure a millionaire like him has his ways. Anyway, we can't do much about it. I didn't think your department or the government would pay it."

"Ha, now you're being a comedian. Call me as soon as you hear something, okay?"

I rang to check on Ricky. He was okay, just frustrated being stuck at home.

"Did you ever get help from anyone else at Cruz's office?" I prodded him.

"No, boss, only Cruz."

"Did you call him on a cellphone?"

"Yes, and I tried the number a few times, but it's disconnected."

"Right. A throw down. Did you have to pay him for information?"

"Sometimes, but mostly it was an exchange of favours, you know the drill, boss."

"Do you know him personally, Ricky?"

"Of course, he was my boss when I was in the force."

"Were you a narc?" I said, surprised.

"Ten years in road patrol, three in the special drug squad."

"Why did you leave?"

"A bust went bad and a cop got killed. I got blamed for messing up."

"Was that cop Pablo Cortez?"

"Yeah, how did you know?"

I played on a hunch. "Ricky, listen to me, this is important... were you in charge of the task force for that bust?"

"Yes, I was."

"So, you took the rap for being in the wrong place to ambush the truck?"

"Yes, and that got Pablo killed," he said, sorrowfully.

"Who told you what gate to be at?"

"My superior operating officer, Vic Cruz."

My phone beeped.

"Hang on, Ricky, I've got another call."

"Hello. Hi, Lola, just a sec, I've got Ricky on hold." I switched back. "Ricky, I've gotta go, it's the Lovejoys, I'll call you back later... but it looks to me like your buddy Cruz is our kidnapper." I switched back. "Lola, sorry... what's up?"

"Dad agreed to take on the debt, so I called Nick Vargas. He's a nice man... he said not to worry and for you to call him to make the arrangements."

"Cool. I'll get onto him."

"Oh, by the way," she remembered, "the kidnapper said he will use MK as his ID when he texts you."

"Okay, sit tight, kiddo, this is the tough part. I'll be in touch."

"Axis."

"Yes."

"Your fee is safe."

"Pleased to hear that, Lola, but it would be safer in my bank account."

"I'll see what I can do. Please be careful."

"I'll do my best, kiddo... bye."

I rang Vargas.

"Nick? It's Axis Stone."

"You must have spoken with Lola?" he said.

"Yeah, so how do you want to play this?" I asked.

"I need to put a few things in place at the bank, and that will take an hour or so. Call me as soon as you get the location."

"Done."

I decided to pack my bag, confident the location for the exchange wouldn't be in Makati. Just then, The Terrible Tango signalled an incoming text. I knew it was the kidnapper — it read: Batangas MK. I had no idea where that was, so I Googled it. Even though it was only a hundred clicks from Makati, that would make it at least a two-hour drive. I'd have to hire a car. I rang Nick back.

"Nick, I've just heard from him. It's a place called Batangas."

"Where in Batangas?" he probed.

"He didn't say... just Batangas."

"What happens next then?" he asked.

He sounded half-hearted, but I pressed on regardless. "Under normal circumstances, I'd have the cops triangulate his cellphone seeing I have his number, but I don't think that would be a wise idea."

"I agree."

"So, I need to get there, text him, and then he'll text me back the final location... obviously somewhere in the area. Is Batangas a big place?"

"Yes... and it's a tough call asking you to drive there and then find the location. Maps are not accurate, and you're a foreigner. I'll take you."

"No, he only wants to deal with me."

"It's my money, Axis. I insist."

"Can't argue with that. Okay, where, when, and how?"

"I will meet you at the helipad on the Peninsula Hotel roof in an hour. We'll fly to Batangas... I'll have a car meet us there."

"Now you're talking."

Nick had raised the bar. I had time to burn, so I called Ricky back.

"Ricky?"

"Boss. I've been thinking about what you said, and I think you're right... Cruz could be our man."

"Yeah, so what convinced you?"

"Something that always bothered me... Cruz is a rich man, not from old money like Vargas, but money he earned as a cop, and as you know, cops get paid a pittance, so how did he get rich? I always believed he was on the take, and I think he was in on that drug bust."

"That would make him partners with Ringo Raye. If Cortez is right, then Ringo is the mastermind."

"Another thing worries me... Bianca Gutierrez was the fiancé of Vargas at the time, and the Vargas family owns and operates ATI, Asian Terminals Inc., where the container holding the drugs was stored."

"Yeah, that's understandable."

"Well, someone had to give the truck access in and out through the high security of the terminal."

"You think that was Bianca?" I questioned.

"It sure makes sense."

"It makes as much sense as someone like Cruz blowing the whistle on Pablo to whoever was in the truck with him, to have him whacked. Two birds with one stone."

"I'm pretty sure I know who was in the truck and killed Pablo."

"Who?"

"Arnel Gutierrez."

Ricky was on the money. It could only be Arnel. That's probably the only reason Bianca had done the dirty on Vargas, to arrange free passage for the truck.

"Maybe Kitty learned the secret and that's why Ringo, Cruz, and the Gutiérrez's need to get rid of her?" I posed.

"And maybe they want their money back from the drugs that went up in smoke first."

"That's it, Ricky, even the figures match, two mill worth of drugs, two mill ransom, now all we need to do is prove it. I'm leaving in a couple of hours to make the exchange."

"Where is it?"

"I can't say, Ricky."

"I understand boss. Just remember they would want Kitty dead. I don't think they'd have any intention of letting her live."

"Good Ricky, I'll take it on advisement. Call you when and if I survive this."

"I hear you, boss. Be careful."

"And listen, if it does go wrong and you don't hear from me by noon tomorrow, call Cortez and tell him everything we've just talked about."

"You can count on me, boss. By the way, you said hitting Pablo was killing two birds with one stone. What did you mean by that?"

"There's more than one reason why Cruz and Raye would want Pablo dead. One was he was going to blow the whistle on Cruz."

"You know that idea adds a very troublesome possibility to this case, boss."

"Yeah, what's that?"

"Cruz would have connections all the way to the president; his task force was appointed directly by him."

"Yeah, so?"

"With that sort of influence, you will need to watch your back. If things don't go Cruz's way, he could call up a favour from someone pretty high up... if you get my drift."

"Roger that, Ricky."

I hung up thinking I'd never been in a spot like this before and it certainly wasn't looking good. The house phone rang and the front desk clerk said they had a Miss Gutierrez in the lobby. I asked for her to be sent up.

Five minutes later, there was a knock at the door. I opened it to find her dressed in a black silk shirt and a white linen skirt; a cute outfit.

"Well," I said. "You finally turn up. Enter."

She came in. I checked the corridor to make sure she was alone — clear, I closed the door.

"I have some questions for you and no buts!" I said, sternly.

She looked at me doubtfully, then caught the full impact of my facial expression.

"Try me," she said, throwing herself down on the couch.

"All I want from you is the truth," I snarled.

She sat back in the sofa with her arms defiantly folded. "Fire away," she grunted.

"Did you arrange permission for the truck to enter and then leave the Asia Container Terminal?"

"Maybe I did, maybe I didn't. What's it to you?"

"Who was in that truck?" I pressed.

"They said on the news it was an undercover cop. He got killed."

"Who was in the truck with him?" I pushed.

"How would I know?" she snapped.

"Who was behind the whole thing?"

"No idea. Look, what's this all about? I came here to tell you something, not to get grilled by you."

I realised I should take it easy on her. But I was running out of time, Vargas was due soon. I pulled up an armchair opposite her and sat. "One last question," I said, eyeballing her. "Did you use me as a diversion at Subic Bay, so that someone could beat up my partner?"

"You said you came alone?"

"Just answer the question."

Her eyes widened with fear. "Um, no."

"Okay, I'm all ears. Spit it out."

"Look, I've probably played my cards wrong up until now, I've had my chances and blown them, big time."

"You mean with Vargas?"

"Yes, and other situations... Sometimes you start with all the right intentions but forces pull you this way and that... and then you wind up doing everything wrong, it all messes up, and there's no going back to fix it."

"You talking about Ringo or Arnel?"

"Whoever, family... people — they can all have an emotional grip on you."

"Okay, go on, I'm listening," I assured her.

"People have been hurt, killed even, and now there's a kidnapping. I feel responsible for starting it all…"

"The entry and exit permit for the truck?"

She started to cry.

"I just don't want anyone else to get hurt, that's all."

I wasn't sure whether to console her or not… maybe that's what she wanted: a shoulder to cry on.

"What are you saying?" I probed, still playing hard-ball.

"I don't want you and Kitty killed."

I stood up.

"Do you know something I don't?" I pressed hard.

"Kitty knows too much, just like me. So, that makes us both targets."

I was getting the picture, and it wasn't pretty, but it was time to leave.

"Why now? Why are you telling me this now?"

She put her face in her hands and wept.

"Look, I've got to go… I've got an important meeting."

She looked up — her eyes red — nose running. "Please don't go, Axis," she pleaded.

"I gave you a chance," I growled, unrelenting. "You admitted nothing, now I'm out of here."

She pulled a face, the nadir of despair. I opened the door for her. She got up and slowly walked towards me. When she reached me, she stood on her tiptoes and gently pecked me on the lips.

"I told you because I'm pregnant. When I told Nick, he asked if I wanted to keep it, I said, no. He knows I have no money…" She started to weep again. "He's such a good guy, Axis… he sent me five thousand dollars to go to Hong Kong for an abortion. I don't want him to know that I'd taken advantage of him, that's all."

"Guilt is a terrible thing, Bianca, but you're going to have to live with that."

I couldn't be bothered to ask the name of the father; I sort of guessed it.

"Can you talk to him for me, Axis?" she pleaded.

"It's time you grew up and sorted out your own life, Bee."

I closed the door behind me, walked her to the elevator and pressed the call button.

"Good luck, kiddo," I said, patting her on the butt into the elevator.

She turned inside and with teary eyes said, "Nothing is what it seems, Axis, don't get yourself killed."

The elevator door closed, leaving me pondering the conundrum: nothing is what it seems?"

CHAPTER FOURTEEN

I **CALLED THE** next elevator, rode it down to the ground, then slipped out of the West Street exit of the Shangri-La. The traffic was heavy, which made it relatively easy to slip between cars on Ayala Avenue to get to the Peninsula Hotel.

The Peninsula's grand lobby made me think I'd been staying in the wrong place, but I didn't have time to linger and went directly to reception. The desk clerk sprang to attention at the mention of the name Vargas, and a boy in a white suit, with matching gloves and a pillbox hat, was immediately summoned to lead me to the rooftop helipad.

We stepped out onto the tarmac just as the Bell 429 touched down. I raced over, ducked under the rotating blades, and climbed onboard the seven-seat chopper.

Nick greeted me with a helmet fitted with coms so we could have a three-way conversation with the pilot. We lifted off.

"My pilot, Dan Ilagan, is ex-military and will provide tactical support for the hand-over," he said.

"Excellent. But we'll need to be careful. The kidnapper is only expecting me."

There came a static-enriched reply from Dan, "No problema."

"I had a visit from Bianca," I said.

With a single raised eyebrow, Nick said, "No coincidence, I heard from her yesterday."

"Yes, I know all about it. But she didn't drop by to tell me just that, she came to warn me."

"Warn you? About what? She wouldn't know about this ... unless—"

"No, I've told nobody. She left me with the conundrum: Nothing is what it seems..."

"What's that supposed to mean?" Nick asked. "She is a bit of a scatter-brain, you know?"

"Yeah, but I think she was trying to tell me the kidnapper plans to kill Kitty and me."

"How would she know that?" Nick asked.

"I got her to admit it was her who arranged access for the truck driven by Pablo Cortez into your security container terminal to pick up a container full of drugs."

"What?" he bleated, shocked.

"Yes, I believe she did it for her brother Arnel, who I suspect was working for Ringo at the time. I also believe Raye was and maybe still is in league with Vic Cruz, head of the special drug force. I think Cruz blew the whistle on Pablo ... the undercover agent driving the truck, who incidentally was the brother of Sancho Cortez ... and sent the drug squad to the wrong gate for the ambush, which resulted in Pablo's murder and two million in drugs going up in flames with the truck."

"My God, do you realise what you're saying?" Vargas shouted, to get above the engine noise.

"I sure do. That puts Cruz directly behind the kidnapping and possibly Raye. I think Kitty knows too much ... the reason they want to take her out, probably as soon as they've banked the ransom."

"It's madness. That means he's definitely planning to kill you as well."

"Sure does ... I think it's how the consortium means to get the two mill back they lost when the dope went up in smoke."

I glanced out of the window at the beautiful countryside below. We were flying over a volcanic crater filled with the bluest water.

"What's that down there?"

"Taal, beautiful isn't it?"

"Yeah, hope I get to see it on the way back."

Nick got the inference.

~ ~ ~

We landed on a helipad at a resort hotel in Anilao, Batangas. Once the rotors had stopped, we deplaned.

We strolled in the warm afternoon sun towards a dark wood-panelled building that was well camouflaged in the tropical vegetation.

"This is Eagle Point Resort, it's owned by a friend of mine," Nick said. "I figured it would make a good HQ. I have a Pajero here, and Dan has arranged three more armed mercenaries. Did you tell Cortez the plan?"

"No. I thought it best not to have any police interference."

"I'm glad you made that decision. You're getting savvy to the ways of us Filipinos, my friend."

"I think survival instinct has caused that," I agreed.

Inside the Nordic style hotel lobby, that made me check around for a Swedish masseuse, we instead found the resort manager, Frank Concepcion, a cultured mestizo Filipino in his mid-fifties with a well-schooled British accent and affable manners. He sent us to a bungalow reserved for Nick. I got the distinct impression Eagle Point was one of Nick's regular haunts: maybe for the odd dirty weekend. The three troopers and Dan were billeted next door in a smaller bungalow.

An hour later, we met up to discuss a strategy. The day felt longer than a state burial, and as the waters of Balayan Bay began to glow with the dying orange embers of the setting sun, so too sank my hopes for a daytime exchange. Just when we were beginning to doubt our actions, The Terrible Tango signalled a text. It was the kidnapper. I read it out to the team … 6043 National Road, Mabini. Money must be in account by 8 P.M., come alone. MK. We studied each other for a moment, contemplating the message.

I checked my watch and asked, "It's six o'clock, is that enough time to get to Mabini?"

"Yes, luckily we're close. It's only fifteen minutes away," Dan said.

"And the money?" I prompted.

"I will need to send a text to my bank manager. The funds will then be transferred immediately," Nick responded.

"Right. I'll notify the Lovejoys, then we'll devise an assault plan."

"Okay, I'll assemble the troops," Dan rumbled.

I went outside to get a better signal and phoned Lola. I told her we were getting set to go in. There wasn't much else I could say. It felt awkward, both of us aware of the consequences of failure. With a tremble of emotion in her voice, she wished me the best of luck.

I went back inside where Nick, Dan, and his three troopers, dressed in night camouflage military fatigues with matching painted faces, were waiting. I felt out of sync dressed in black jeans, my favourite T, and Nike black/hyper punch/photo blue/anthracite trainers, but hey, I guess it was my show after all, and I could dress how I liked.

We carried out weapon checks, and then Dan displayed a topographical map of the area on his laptop.

"This is the target ... we will use the Pajero along the driveway up to the house until here," he said, gruffly. "Then we will deploy and go in on foot ... Nick will accompany Axis to the house."

He changed the picture to a satellite image.

"The photo was taken fifteen minutes ago. As you can see, there is no life to be seen anywhere." He triggered an infrared filter and six stationary figures appeared in red and he continued, "Can't see what's inside the house, but note the hostiles holed up around it ... they will be our targets."

"How should we play this, Nick?" I asked.

"I'll hide under a thermo blanket in the rear of the Pajero, to avoid detection. Once you're inside the house, I'll find a way to follow you in."

"The kidnapper will be set up to detonate the bomb by cellphone," Dan said, matter-of-factly. "Theoretically, he will be a distance away but with the house in sight, or positioned for a relayed message. We expect he will wait until he has the money and for Axis to be inside, before he detonates the bomb."

"So, I have to let it go down to the wire before I transfer the money," Nick admitted, gravely.

"Exactly, Nick," Dan said. "Meantime, we will knock over his support hand to hand. It will be risky, they will have orders to signal the kidnapper at the first sign of trouble."

He had an excited expression, obviously enjoyed his gig. He'd made it perfectly clear how tough it was going to be. The possibility of being blown to bits made me nauseous.

"Will you be able to handle this, Stone?" Dan asked.

The question put me on the spot — my Aussie bravado kicked in — I gulped, "Yeah mate, too late to chicken-out now."

"It is not now that I am worried about, Stone ... it is when you see Kitty sitting on a time bomb," Dan said, eyeballing me. "That is when you will have the weird feeling of having to make a decision that could well end your own life."

I could see what he was getting at and it wasn't pretty.

"I can hack it," I said, with a fake confident smirk.

"Any questions?" Dan said, eyeing us. There were none.

~ ~ ~

Butterflies were fluttering in my stomach by the time Nick and the others took cover in the car, giving the illusion that I was alone. I provided a continuous commentary all the way there, and just as I began to relax, Dan's voice emerged from behind me.

"The driveway entrance should be up ahead on your left," he said.

"Roger that," I confirmed.

The rolling hills cascaded in a series of graceful curves down to Balayan Bay, perhaps a couple of clicks away. Midway, a house sat atop a hill, its driveway winding up to it. The gaunt turrets and spires of the house cut a sinister silhouette against the night sky, reminiscent of the opening shot of a horror movie.

"Got it, I'm turning into the driveway," I reported.

"Pull up when you can get under tree cover. Get out, walk into the headlights, and check the map in them," Dan instructed.

Navigating the narrow, shadowy driveway was a challenge. A full moon was ascending from the Bay, enhancing the eeriness. I parked the Pajero under a large tree, disembarked, and followed Dan's instructions. Meanwhile, Dan and his men silently exited the vehicle and disappeared into the darkness.

As I looked up, the old, two-story Spanish hacienda, with its red terracotta-tiled roof, starkly contrasted against the moonlight. It was dark inside. With the diversion completed and the troops deployed, I returned to the Pajero and drove to the old house's forecourt. As I stepped out, I reached for my pistol — a weapon tends to stabilize the nerves somewhat.

The kidnapper had chosen the location astutely. It was secluded, dilapidated, and neglected — it seemed it had been vacant for decades. The tropical trees around the house cast ominous shadows in the moonlight.

Approaching the decayed front door, which was unhinged and slightly ajar, I realized the challenging part was yet to come — where was she? I entered the dark foyer and scrutinized for signs of life. The inside was even more run-down than the outside. A once stately wooden balustrade leading to the second floor had been nearly stripped of its timber long ago. Moonlight streamed through the broken roof tiles, illuminating gaping holes in the floor where floorboards had been removed. Just another obstacle I'd have to navigate in the dark. Suddenly, I heard a 'psst' from behind. It was Nick — his camouflage was so effective that he seemed like a mere phantom from twenty feet away. It was comforting to know he was there for backup. He tossed me a penlight, which allowed me to continue with increased confidence. Stepping over chasms, which I assumed led to the basement, I noticed recent drag marks and footprints in the dusty floor. The tracks led through a pair of feeble doors barely hanging from rusted hinges, leading to what appeared to be a dining room. I followed the tracks to the doors and gingerly pried open the most stable one — it creaked and groaned in protest but yielded. Once inside the room, I stopped abruptly, careful not to swallow too hard as my heart pounded in my throat.

In the room's centre, bathed in a pool of moonlight streaming down through a gap in the ceiling from two floors above, sat an old wooden chair. In it was a naked female — Kitty. She was blindfolded and unconscious, her chin resting on her chest. Her arms were tied behind the chair, and her ankles were secured to the chair's rear legs. As soon as I saw the bomb under the chair, Dan's prediction came true: my nerves kicked into high gear. The penlight flickered in my trembling hand as I attempted to scan the rest of the room. The light flashed on two cameras positioned high up, causing me to freeze. I pocketed the light and remained still in the doorway. Suddenly, something touched my shoulder, and I jumped.

"Ugh!" I gasped.

"It's only me ... are you all right?" Nick whispered.

"Yeah, two cameras ... ten o'clock and two ... we're out of shot here. Are you set to make the transfer?"

"I see them," he replied, producing a device.

"What's that?" I queried.

"A G5 cellular phone jammer ... it has a radius of twenty meters. It will buy us a thirty-second window."

"Window? What window? Explain, please."

He brought out a knife and spoke very deliberately. "I will cut her free ... you pick her up and carry her out of here."

The idea of carrying a limp body all that distance seemed absurd for a guy like me, whose idea of exercise is occasionally choosing the stairs over the elevator.

"You've got to be kidding, man!" I protested. "They'll be cleaning us off the walls with a mop!"

"Maybe, maybe not ... follow me," he retorted.

CHAPTER FIFTEEN

N ICK DIDN'T GIVE me time to debate it any further. He just took off like a rocket. When he reached her, he dropped the jammer beside the chair and immediately began hacking away at the ropes binding her wrists. I raced over beside him, puffing like I'd just run a marathon. Hastily, I slipped my arm around her and took her weight on my shoulder. With her hands free, she slumped against me. Nick knelt down behind her and started on her ankle binds. I tensed up, ready to take all of her weight. I didn't notice any obvious signs of abuse on her body. Bloody hell, I was earning my fee on this one. I hoped the seconds weren't counting down as fast as my heart was thumping.

"Go!" Nick cried out.

I quickly slid my free hand under her legs and lifted her in my arms like a baby — a very heavy baby — and then I took off out of there. Nick was close behind; I could hear his footsteps drumming loudly on the wooden floor. Without the help of the penlight, I had no idea where the cavities in the floor were. I got through the doorway and suddenly felt my left leg go from under me. I'd gone through a bloody great hole in the floor. We stopped with an agonizing jolt — my arms and Kitty's legs preventing us from falling completely through. I don't know how, but I managed to hang on to her. I felt like the impact had dislocated both my shoulders. Lucky she was unconscious. If she'd been awake and rigid, we would have ended up all busted in the basement for sure. Nick appeared, and straining, he managed to lift us out of the cavity. Then came an almighty explosion. Just as I drew my legs out of the hole, the shockwave hit me with a force that sent me sliding across the floor on my backside — it was as though the hand of God had given me one almighty shove. My ears were ringing like church bells. Kitty was no longer in my arms. I looked up and immediately ducked down flat on the floorboards to get under a massive fireball that roared out of the living room and passed overhead. Instinctively, I curled up into a foetal position, knowing there was more coming. And I was right — a wind hit me hard, carrying with it a salvo of debris. When I felt the explosion had passed, I blinked my eyes open and sat up, wondering how much of me was left. The air was thick with dust. The lounge room was ablaze in thick orange flames. I could just make out two motionless dark figures sprawled out on the floor. Out of the smoke, hands grabbed me and lifted me up by the arms. I was carried at speed out through the front door — it was surreal — I thought it must have been angels extracting me from the fires of hell. No, wait, why would they do that? I'm agnostic … that would mean … oh dear, maybe this was proof of divinity. Was I having an out of body experience? I hope so … if I live, I can write the book. Where's the bright light? Then, I saw it. There was a bright light at the end of the tunnel! It passed, only to be replaced by another, then another. I squinted to focus and recognised oyster light fittings and realized I was on my back, looking up at ceiling lights flitting past. My hearing returned somewhat, and I could hear squeaking and rolling sounds — then I knew it was a hospital trolley. I was being wheeled fast along a corridor. I sat bolt upright … and then darkness consumed me.

Voices … I opened my eyes, alerted by them … one sounded familiar … it was Cortez. He saw I was awake and leaned over my hospital bed to speak.

"How do you feel, Stone?"

His voice was distant, but I could understand.

"Like something the cat dragged in," I groaned through parched lips. "Where am I?"

"Makati Med, you were injured in your rescue mission."

I tried to move, but my shoulders ached like hell.

"And the others?" I asked.

"Vargas is in a private suite upstairs … naturally. Kitty is with him. She's on life support … he has superficial injuries like yours."

"Will she be all right?"

"Touch and go … she took some shrapnel."

"I'm surprised we survived."

"You were lucky to have Ilagan and his men get you out. Apparently, the house burnt down in no time flat."

I counted the lumps in my bed. "Am I all here?"

"Ah, you took some splinters in the right arm … but you'll live. You can get up if you like."

It felt stupid being in a hospital bed for an injury so minor, so I struggled up.

"Your clothes are in the closet," he said.

I opened it and was disappointed to find my best T-shirt torn to shreds.

"Damn!" I complained, as I stripped off the hospital gown and pulled on my jeans. Then I put on what was left of the T. I picked up my gun.

"You don't have a permit for that?"

"So? Call the police," I joked.

I went into the en-suite bathroom and splashed water on my face. Checked the mirror, there were small lacerations all over my face and forearms. My shoulders ached like hell when I tried to raise my arms – but I'd live. I found a toothbrush and paste, so used them.

"Just how bad are they?" I called out to Sancho, who was still perched on the edge of the bed.

"Vargas is up and about. Like you, he only sustained minor cuts and bruises, but the girl took a nasty hit … some flying debris hit her in the head and peppered her body … no clothes to protect her either. You should have told me you were going to make the exchange."

I came out and eyeballed him. "Sancho, I couldn't take the risk … I was acting on instructions from the family, you know that."

That riled him up. He jumped off the bed, pointed his finger threateningly, and shouted, "Just who gave you permission to go on a rampage around the countryside like a vigilante death squad trying to rescue a damsel in distress?"

I returned serve with verve, "Nick Vargas and his two million bucks, that's who! Let's get something straight here, Chief Inspector … the most likely suspect in the kidnapping of Kitty Lovejoy and the murder of Chiki Dee is an untouchable cop, one of yours. So, the real question is: with only hours before the ransom deadline, would you have risked saving Kitty's life by informing the cops with dubious integrity of the plan?"

"No. I expect you might be right, Stone, but after what happened, I think you have only created a bigger and more dangerous problem than you originally had."

"And why would that be? We've got the victim back for Christ's sake," I argued.

"Because Vargas didn't pay the ransom and the kidnapper failed to kill you and Kitty … so, she remains a target for whatever it is she knows and you for what you might find out."

"Oh shit!" I gasped, wide-eyed.

I needed to pay Nick a visit to unload on him. We rode the elevator together to the ninth-floor Presidential suites, where Sancho led the way along a narrow corridor. Two uniforms posted outside the door singled out the correct room. A nod from Sancho earned us entry. It was a fancy setup, more like a hotel penthouse than a hospital room … reserved for the rich, obviously. Nick was sitting in an armchair dressed in casual attire, reading a newspaper, a dozen or so plasters decorating his face, neck and hands.

He lowered the paper and raised an eyebrow. "Axis, you need another T-shirt," he said light-heartedly. He could tell by the look on my face I was dirty. "Ah, you obviously know by now that I didn't pay the ransom and you're pissed, right?"

118

"You're damn right I'm pissed. Nice to see you too, Nick," I spat, with as much cynicism as I could muster. His face exhibited similar bomb residual to mine. I sat down opposite him. "You of course chose not to tell me because you preferred to risk my life than be upfront," I snarled.

"I wasn't sure you'd understand. Winston Lovejoy came up with the idea."

"What? ... Good for him ... and so that makes it right, does it? Good to know who you can trust." I stood. "Well, that puts an end to this job, it's time for me to present an invoice and get out of Dodge. Goodbye, Vargas, nice knowing you."

I stormed out of the room. Sancho gave chase and stopped me in the corridor. "Stone! Wait. You can't quit now, my friend, the job is only half done. We still have to catch the bastard or he'll get away with it."

I turned and got in his face. "So now I'm your friend. Look, it isn't my problem anymore, pal."

"But what if Kitty dies? What about Chiki Dee?"

"Man, one minute you're reprimanding me for breaking police protocol and the next you're pleading with me to stay on the case. What is it with you Filipinos, you don't trust anyone ... including each other?"

"I guess it looks like I am in two minds, my friend, but if you are right and Cruz is behind this, then it will take the three of us to nail him."

"I don't know, Vargas could've got me killed. He used me and I don't like being used."

"He also saved your life," he said, resting a consoling hand on my shoulder. "He was only doing what he could to save Kitty. You would probably have done the same thing ... wouldn't you?"

"Yeah, maybe," I reluctantly agreed.

"Look, you have every right to go back home and leave the case with us, my friend, but I think you have more integrity than that. I know using that word sounds weird coming from a Filipino cop, but we're not all bent. Some of us take pride in what we do."

"I didn't realise you had a sense of humour."

"Only when I laugh," he said, his gold tooth glimmering in his smile.

He'd convinced me to bat on, but we needed to put together a fresh strategy, so we went back to consult Nick. Sancho believed the kidnapper would make a move to kill Kitty once he discovered she'd survived the bomb, and the same would probably apply to me. It would be easier to keep Kitty a secret than me. My answer to that was to use me as bait to lure him in, but Sancho wasn't about to agree.

"It is far too easy to have someone hit in the Philippines," he said sternly. "All a bent cop needs to do is have a jailed killer released from prison for a couple of hours for a hit in exchange for money or favours."

"Yeah, I guess so," I allowed.

"A hit only costs five thousand pesos, Axis," Nick added.

"A hundred bucks ... life's cheap here, no wonder it's tough for you cops."

"If you saw our pay packet you'd be shocked."

"He'd get less than two hundred bucks a week," Nick said, referring to Sancho.

"That's probably the gas allowance for an Aussie senior investigator," I submitted. "But I still reckon I'd make the ideal bait."

We agreed to sleep on it and then meet up again to discuss a new plan. In the meantime, I was warned to watch my butt and not trust anybody — after what had just happened, that sounded somewhat hypocritical.

CHAPTER SIXTEEN

W HEN I GOT back to the Shang, I needed to call Lola. I was pissed that Winston had made a sly deal with Nick that had put me in danger, so I rang them to dump on them, and was surprised when Winston answered the phone. "Winston, Stone here... just the man I wanted to speak to... Kitty? She's in intensive care, why ask me how she is, seems you've got a tighter bond with Vargas? Listen to me, the lousy fee you're paying me doesn't include getting blown to bits... no that doesn't come with the job... staying alive does... I resent being used, especially by my own client. I'll tell you what I mean... you did a bloody side deal with Vargas not to pay the ransom and I should have been told about it. Sure, I still would've gone in. Anyhow, that's ancient history, make me a better deal or I'm out of here. Yes, okay, that sounds reasonable..." Appeased, I changed my tone. "I want half in my account ASAP and the rest on completion. Good. Incidentally, why did you answer Lola's phone? She's what?"

We ended the call.

Still choking on the news from old man Lovejoy, I grabbed a towel and went down for a dip in the pool. I phoned Ricky from poolside and was glad to hear he'd recovered enough to return to the case. We arranged to meet in the morning for breakfast by the pool. There was little to keep me at poolside that time of day, all the talent was strutting its stuff to Makati's trendiest bars for happy hour. I went back to my room to shower and just stepped out when the door buzzer sounded. I went into the bedroom, pulled on a robe, collected the .38 from the top drawer of the bedroom bureau, and slipped it into the side pocket that sagged a little under the weight. What the hell? I figured I preferred to be sartorially dead than the real thing. Then, I went to the door, and feeling real brave, opened it a couple of inches. Standing there resplendent in a little black Chanel number was beautiful Lola.

"Did I get you out of bed, Axis?" she purred.

"No, only the shower," I smiled. "Come in."

Her dark eyes smouldered a little while she cased the room expecting to find a naked female.

"Let me make you a drink," I said.

"I'd like that." She gave me a long look of appraisal. "Is all that hair on your chest for real, Axis?"

"It has to go back in the morning," I joked. "I get a reduced rate for nightly rentals from a little old wigmaker who grows mushrooms in the hotel basement."

I made for the bar fridge and mixed a couple of drinks.

"Hope you like rye." I handed her one, then sat in an armchair with mine and raised my glass to her. "Cheers. Welcome to Manila."

She sat opposite on the couch, crossed her shapely legs and offered her glass.

"Thanks, cheers big ears."

"All the better to hear you with," I scoffed.

"So, how's Kitty?"

"Ask your buddy, Nick?"

"Why?"

"Because you and Winston sold me out, that's why."

"What are you saying?"

"You had me risk my life by not paying the ransom and Nick not telling me. That's no way to treat your beloved colleague. More like an enemy," I remonstrated.

"That wasn't any of my doing, I knew nothing about it... I would never..."

"Don't sell me any bullshit lady."

She got up and cruised over to me catlike as if on a cloud and then slid onto my lap. She pouched her ruby red lips, gently pressed them against mine and then eyeballed me up close — real close.

"I wouldn't get you hurt... honest," she half-groaned.

Then she kissed me.

~ ~ ~

In the morning, I climbed out of the sack and, hastily dressing, finished my own drink in two gulps and hers in three. The kidnapper would know by now that Kitty Lovejoy had been rescued and was in a coma at a private hospital. That would attract him like a moth to a flame. It was time to make the next move. I quickly wrote a note telling Lola to stay in the room. It was critical to keep her presence in Manila a secret, as she could easily become a secondary target for the kidnapper. I said, 'I'll call you in the room at 10 A.M.,' and then I rode the elevator down to meet Ricky at the poolside.

He was waiting when I arrived. The humidity suggested a storm was on its way.

"Hey Ricky, good to see you back on deck," I said, taking a seat under the umbrella.

"Thanks, boss... I heard on the news about the rescue and Miss Kitty in a coma. You look like you took some shrapnel. He will still come to get her, you know. Probably send somebody else. Did he get the ransom?"

"No."

"Why? What happened?"

"At the last minute, the family chose not to pay," I growled.

"Then you better watch your back, boss. The kidnapper will blame you for that."

"Other than retribution and being out of pocket, what do you think is driving this guy?"

"I think Kitty must know something incriminating. Maybe she saw his face... knows him even. Or maybe she knows something about the murder of Pablo Cortez."

"Yeah, well, she did spend time with Ringo Raye, so there is no telling what she knows. Boy, it's muggy."

"There's a typhoon coming."

"When?"

"It will probably hit tonight... it's a big one. Have you been in a typhoon before?"

"We get southerly busters in Sydney and the odd tornado, but as I understand it, they're nothing compared to what you guys get here."

"So, it will be a new experience for you."

"One I could do without, Ricky. We've got enough on our plate without worrying about bloody Mother Nature."

I checked my watch. "Okay, let's order up... we need to be at the hospital in two hours. Can you drive?"

He held up the plaster cast on his right hand. "Lucky I am left-handed. No worries, boss."

After we'd indulged ourselves on an assortment of Shangri-La culinary delights and copious cups of freshly brewed coffee, we were caffeine wired and ready to go. The Terrible Tango sounded... it was Cortez.

"Sancho, what's up?"

"A short while ago, I received a phone call from the office of the Mayor of Makati," he said with a solemn tone.

"Okay... and?"

"His office was asking about you."

"Me?" I said, surprised. "I didn't know I was so popular."

"It's my guess you will soon get a call from Mayor Rodriguez."

"Hmm, this isn't sounding good."

"I would say someone has pulled some strings from up high to stop the investigation now that you have Kitty back."

"Has he shut you down?"

"You could say that. But you're regarded as the loose cannon, my friend."

"Yes, I can understand that... you can be shut down, but I can't."

"Exactly."

"What's your advice, Sancho?"

"My investigation into the murder of Chiki Dee can't be shut down, it's ongoing, but they know it's a dead end. I have been reminded that Kitty Lovejoy is a foreigner and that finding her kidnapper isn't a priority."

"That smacks of it becoming a racist cold case."

"It sure does," he said, dispiritedly.

"Tell me Sancho, does this Mayor Rodriguez have the capacity to run me out of town?"

"Absolutely," he said, emphatically.

"And you can't help me?"

"Only if you want to spend time in a prison cell."

"No thanks, it's not my favourite smell! So, either I talk to this guy or avoid him?"

"That decision is yours, my friend, but my advice is to talk to him. I don't want you run out of town. As I see it, you are the best chance we've got of rounding up these criminals."

"Hey, flattery will get you everywhere," I said perkily.

"How's Ricky?" he asked.

"He's right here with me... back on the case."

"Good, then ask him about Rodriguez, he knows a lot about him."

"Okay, will do. Talk later."

I hung up and looked over my sunglasses at Ricky sitting opposite me.

"Did you get the drift of that conversation?"

"Yes, you're to expect a call from Mayor Rodriguez and Cortez has been shut down, the case has gone cold."

"You've got it in one. So, tell me about this dude Rodriguez?"

"Okay boss, before I joined the force I worked for him in security. He was running for mayor of Ermita back then."

"When was this?" I asked.

"End of the eighties. Back then, Ermita was like P. Burgos is today but with many more bars. Rodriguez got voted in as mayor because he promised to get rid of the bars. I was part of the task force to close them down."

"Sounds like a tough gig."

"It was very tough... mainly because the fifty or so bars were operated by foreigners, Australians, Americans, a couple from the Netherlands. They were all gangsters in one way or another — it was serious prostitution — lots of money being made from the heavy traffic of American military personnel, tourists and lots of rig-pigs on furlough from offshore oil rigs. Anyway, to cut a long story short, it turned into a street war... and we were on the losing side. That's when Rodriguez pulled his trump card: the bar owners didn't own the freehold to their bars, they only leased the premises from Filipinos. Rodriguez got to each and every property owner, bought the properties from them and then evicted the bar owners. It was all done quickly before they could even realize what was happening, and by the time they did, it was too late."

"He's got guts... that wouldn't have gone down well."

"He was only saved from being hit because he cut a deal with the biggest bar owners to move to P. Burgos Street in Makati, where they still are today. Rodriguez then developed the Ermita properties and made millions. The irony is that two years ago, he was voted mayor of Makati but hasn't tried to clean up P. Burgos Street, like he did in Ermita, they say because of the deal he'd struck."

"He sold his soul to the devil, huh? Do you think that deal was with Ringo Raye?"

"Raye didn't have a bar in Ermita, but he bought into P. Burgos Street at the very same time Rodriguez became mayor of Makati."

"What a coincidence."

"Many believe way too much of a coincidence."

"So, let's assume he's in bed with Raye, he might also be in bed with Cruz?"

"That's very possible because he and Cruz were amigos back in the Ermita days, and many people wondered how Rodriguez got the money to buy out all of those properties."

"Could have been drug money from Cruz?"

"A big chance, boss."

"So, Ricky, how should I deal with this guy when he rings?"

"Very, very carefully, boss. He is not a man to be messed with... he is more dangerous than Raye and Cruz put together."

"I hear you... You know an old friend of mine in the force once taught me that buying time on a case is good, it makes the bad guys sweat." I held up my smartphone and turned it off. "There, I'll talk to him when I'm good and ready. In the meantime, we've got a job to do."

CHAPTER SEVENTEEN

THE VALET DELIVERED Ricky's Corolla to the Shang forecourt and we hopped in.

"Where are we going boss?"

"St. Luke's in Quezon City."

The traffic on EDSA Boulevard was fearsome, so I reclined in the seat to grab a short nap. Ricky woke me twenty minutes later.

"Boss, there's a bike tailing us and I don't like it."

I quickly sat up in the seat and adjusted the passenger side mirror for a better rear-view. Sure enough, a Yamaha FZ16 was right on our tail.

"Can you lose him Ricky?"

"Not in this traffic boss."

"Are you certain he's trouble?"

"Just my instinct tells me. I'll turn into the next street and see if he follows."

"Good idea."

Ricky hit the blinkers and took the next street on the right. We both checked the rear vision mirrors.

"He is following us," Ricky said dolefully.

I sighted a gas station up ahead.

"Drive into that gas station and out the other side then head back the way we were coming."

Ricky got the idea and drove slowly up to a pump. The biker followed. Once the bike had stopped, Ricky hit the gas and we screeched out onto the road. He made a quick turn and sped back toward Ortigas leaving the bike in our dust. When we reached Ortigas, Ricky squeezed into the line of traffic. I checked behind — the biker was about six cars back and had pulled out to pass them to catch up to us. "He's coming," I warned Ricky. I pulled my gun and held it on my lap ready. "Damn it! We'll have to confront him. Can you handle it?"

"Not much choice is there, boss?"

"No, okay, turn into the next side street and stop."

I braced myself ready to shoot him when he pulled up beside us. Ricky turned off Ortigas into Frontera Drive, and stopped.

"He's coming fast!" Ricky shrieked. "Get down!"

The bike roared up on my side of the car. I wasn't expecting that, I figured it would be the driver's side... it all happened in slow motion — I ducked — he unloaded a clip into the car. Head down, I shielded my face from the shower of glass from the shattering windows. I huddled as low in the seat as I could, hoping he wasn't reloading, and then popped up to take a shot at him ... I was too late ... the bike sped off. Ricky was in the driver's side well ... I patted him on the head.

"You can come up now mate, he's gone."

But Ricky didn't move. I looked at the palm of my hand ... it was smeared with blood ... Ricky had taken a head shot — he was dead. In shock, I pulled out my phone, switched it on, and phoned Cortez. I don't even know what I said but within half an hour there were blue strobe lights flashing and sirens sounding. The chaos of them arriving brought me back to reality and I realised I was sitting on the kerb beside the bullet riddled Corolla in a daze, traumatized by the attack and the loss of my friend.

Sancho led me over to his black Nissan X-trail, sat me on the back seat, and put a flask of brandy in my trembling hand. I took a big swig, and then sank down with my head in my hands. Sancho placed a consoling hand on my shoulder ... everything we were doing suddenly felt futile. I was responsible for Ricky and Chiki, they were good people and didn't deserve to be killed by these bastards. At a time like this I questioned everything I was doing — was it worth it?

"What can I say Axis, this is Manila," Sancho said, sympathetically. "This was always going to happen. Did you speak with Rodriguez?"

"No, I turned my phone off, I'll speak with him when I'm good and ready."

"That might have been a bad move, Axis."

I got the inference and hated it.

On the way to St. Luke's with Cortez, I phoned Lola and told her what had happened. The news terrified her. She agreed to stay put at the Shangri-La and remain vigilant, but she was scared — very scared. The scary thing for me was that there had been no missed call: Rodriguez hadn't phoned — meaning Ricky's murder was probably a warning from him. Cortez certainly seemed to think so.

The plan was to use the suite at St. Luke's as a ruse to ensnare the kidnapper. All the while Kitty was secretly on life support at Makati Medical Hospital. Nick and I would take up armed vigilance at St. Luke's. We expected the kidnapper to believe Kitty was hospitalized there after we'd issued a false news report to all media. By the hit on Ricky, the ruse had worked, but it had cost him his life.

We rode the elevator up to the private suites on the top floor of Tower One, then entered past two uniformed guards posted outside the room. We found Nick on the phone. He quickly ended the call and jumped up from the armchair when he saw my face and the blood spatter on my jacket.

"Axis! What the hell happened!"

We filled him in including the story on Rodriguez.

He slumped back into the armchair with his head in his hands. "These assholes are getting the better of us," he groaned.

"My actions have cost another life," I admitted.

"I'm sorry you lost your friend, Axis," Nick said sincerely.

Losing Ricky hurt deep down in my guts and I could feel the bile of reprisal rising. My mission had now taken on a new face: I wasn't going to rest until I got the bastards that killed my friend. Ricky had taken a fatal bullet for me — I owed him to get even.

"I can feel your angst Axis and I sympathize with you but you can't let it blind you," Nick said compassionately.

"Don't worry Axis you'll get your shot at getting even," Sancho said, in a tone that felt like he'd given the same speech before.

I nodded slowly and met his gaze. "I hear you Sancho," I said, knowing that hard cold hate had taken hold of my purpose.

Just as Sancho was leaving, he got a call from a doctor at Makati Med … it was good news … Kitty was out of the coma. The news radically changed our plans.

"Does the hit on Ricky reopen the case, Sancho?" I asked sternly.

"Sure does," he growled.

It was crucial to converse with Kitty to understand why she was being targeted. Sancho steered us to Makati Med with lights flashing and the siren blaring, reaching speeds that would have made a race car driver blush. En route, we picked up Lola from the Shang. Disguised masterfully, she quietly slipped into the car at a secure exit, typically reserved only for dignitaries and celebrities evading the press or overzealous fans. Upon arriving at Makati Med, it was clear that security was high — a lot was riding on this.

A nurse escorted us past a pair of uniformed guards and into the Presidential suite, where Kitty was lying in bed. This was my first encounter with her while she was conscious. Lola crossed the room in a flash, enveloping her sister in an embrace. Observing them together, I noticed their striking resemblance — almost identical, save for the hair colour: Lola blonde, Kitty red.

After allowing the sisters a moment, Nick took his turn. With the emotional reunions out of the way, it was time to address Kitty with some pressing questions.

The absence of make-up accentuated the pallor of her face. Her eyes were red-rimmed and swollen, her lips chapped, yet a spark in her eyes signalled she was maintaining control. I perched on the edge of the bed and met her bloodshot gaze.

"Hey Kitty, I'm Axis Stone, a private investigator from Sydney. I've been working on your kidnapping case."

"Yeah, they told me you saved me from the explosion. You put your life on the line for me," she rasped, managing a pained smile. "I can't thank you enough."

She clasped my hand, her weak grip revealing her frailty.

"I know you need rest, but it's important for me to ask you some questions. Can you handle it?"

Tears began to well up in her eyes as she nodded in agreement.

"Did you catch a glimpse of your kidnapper or anyone else involved?"

She shook her head, indicating a no.

"What about when you were given a phone to speak with your family?"

"No, I was blindfolded."

"Okay. Is there anything else you can provide that might help us identify your kidnappers or the place where you were held?"

Closing her eyes tightly as if to recollect, tears leaked from under her long, black eyelashes. Her face contorted in pain; I was unsure if it was due to her physical wounds or the emotional trauma of her kidnapping. Suddenly, her swollen eyes sprang open.

"Gum, my gum," she exclaimed.

"Gum?" I asked, seeking clarification.

"I spent most of the time on a boat. I could hear water lapping, birds..." she paused to clear her throat with a cough. "I also heard footsteps on the deck above me. I was kept naked, blindfolded, drugged... it's all just a terrible blur."

"You mentioned gum?" I prodded.

"When they took me, they filled me up with drugs. I woke up tied to a chair, blindfolded and naked. I could feel the air prickling my skin... I still had my chewing gum in my mouth."

Behind me, Lola let out an affectionate snicker — chewing gum must've been one of Kitty's quirks.

"A guy came in and took me to a tiny toilet to pee. I took out the gum and stuck it under the toilet seat. It should still be there. From then on, the same guy brought me a bucket to use. He also cleaned me with a sponge. By then, I recognised him by his strong body odour."

"It must've been a nightmare... did they feed you?" Lola inquired.

"The same guy spoon-fed me. He never spoke. To be honest, I have no idea what else he got up to. After each feed, he'd inject me with something... I was practically unconscious all the time... that's why it's all such a blur."

Just as I was about to question her about why she might be a target, a stern nurse barged into the room, demanding us to leave. Kitty needed to rest, and this nurse, who seemed like she could have been a high-ranking officer in the SS under Heinrich Himmler, was not to be trifled with. We complied and made our way back to my hotel to strategize our next move.

~ ~ ~

There were four of us in my room. It was apparent that Nick was completely smitten with Lola. After all, she was the spitting image of Kitty and, in my biased opinion, even more attractive.

"I suggest we abandon the St. Luke's entrapment and focus on the chewing gum clue," I proposed.

"We'll need to send the gum to Australia for DNA analysis," Nick added.

"That won't be necessary, Sancho," I countered. "We simply need to find the gum under the toilet seat in the boat to implicate the owner."

"That means we have three boats to search at Subic Marina," Nick pointed out.

"Will we need a search warrant, Sancho?" I asked, hoping the answer would be no.

He rubbed his furrowed brow, a look of worry crossing his weathered face. "If I apply for a warrant and the kidnapper is who we think he is, Cruz, he will find out and..."

"The boat will just sail off into the sunset," Nick finished for him.

"That doesn't leave us with many options or much time," I concluded.

"It sounds extremely dangerous to me," Lola expressed with genuine concern.

To me, it felt like a lay down misère. From the beginning, I'd been suspicious of Ringo. "I'm betting on Raye's boat, Bodyshot," I announced confidently. "Who's up for a drink?"

We raided the mini-bar, which had thankfully been restocked while I was out. It was nearly empty by the time we finished, but at least we had a plan. At 3 p.m., Nick would have Dan fly us to Subic Bay via helicopter for the three of us to carry out the raid. Sancho wouldn't participate because it had to be an unofficial operation. If we found the chewing gum evidence on Bodyshot, we were to call Sancho immediately. He would be on standby to raid Ringo's apartment and arrest him for suspected kidnapping under article 267 of Philippine law.

CHAPTER EIGHTEEN

I SAW NICK and Sancho out and then turned my attention to Lola. "It's after lunchtime, I feel like something to eat. You hungry?"

The Terrible Tango sounded.

"Love the ringtone," Lola said.

Speak of the devil — it was Raye on the line.

"Ringo," I said loud for Lola to know.

"Stone, haven't heard from you in a while, thought you might be dead."

"Not if I have anything to do with it."

"Heard you got Kitty back but she's in a coma. What's the prognosis?"

"Could be days or weeks before she comes out of it, no-one knows. Tell me something, do you know Vic Cruz?" I pressed.

"Cruz you say, hmm, don't know … name rings a bell."

"Yeah, I can hear it chiming from here."

"What's that supposed to mean?" he snapped.

"Not a lot but the name keeps cropping up."

"Yeah, in relation to what?"

"Um, drugs, murder, kidnapping, you know, that sort of thing," I said casually.

"Can't help you Stone, I've told you that before."

I could tell by his tone he'd say no more.

I asked the leading question. "Ricky Esposo got hit this morning, have you heard?"

"No. You telling me he's dead?"

"A shooter on a bike tried to take us out and Ricky got hit," I said, angrily.

"Sorry to hear that."

I pushed further, "Tell me about Rodriguez?"

"Who?"

"The Mayor."

There was a pregnant pause, then he asked, "What the hell's he got to do with this?"

"That's what I'm trying to find out."

"More importantly, where's Kitty? I want to pay her a visit," he said, quickly changing the subject.

"Like I said, she hasn't got much to say at the moment, but when she does, I promise, you'll be one of the first to know."

"That sounds sarcastic Stone, you've either got yourself an attitude problem or I'm imagining it."

"Comes with the gig."

"Yours or mine?"

"Probably both."

"Was the ransom paid?" he asked.

"No, so that's fifteen love to the good guys."

"Watch your serve Stone … Catch you round."

He didn't seem very pleased with my rhetoric and abruptly terminated the call. I didn't mind, my aim was to make him nervous by putting him on notice.

"I can tell by your body language that was intimidating," Lola said.

"Kitty's ex and big-time local gangster … Ringo Raye … it's his boat we going to hit tonight. If we find what we're after, he'll be facing life for kidnapping."

"What makes you think he'll stay in town after what you just told him?"

"When I mentioned Cruz and Rodriguez, he knew it was checkmate. Now he's only got two options left … run or fight … and knowing him … he'll fight."

"Are you saying he'll try and kill you and Kitty?"

"He already tried this morning and poor Ricky took the bullet."

She shrieked, "Was that him? I thought it was the other guy … the mayor?"

"They're all in it together, Raye, Rodriguez and Cruz. None of them personally the shooter, but one of them sure as eggs arranged it."

"I'm confused … and that doesn't make me feel very secure with all of this."

I gave her a hug.

"We have to try and stay one step ahead of these bastards, kid."

She stared deep into my eyes and I watched the tears welling up.

"Is Kitty safe where she is?"

"Safer than us, we're keeping the deception going that she's at St. Luke's, just as an added precaution."

I checked my timepiece.

"It's time to go," I said.

"Please don't get yourself killed," she whimpered.

"I don't have time for that," I chuckled, jokingly. Deep down inside I knew she was right — this could all end up nasty. "Don't go anywhere and don't answer the door or the phone, okay?"

She nodded. I could see the fear in her eyes.

~ ~ ~

Having done it before, it only took a few minutes for me to hightail it across Ayala to the Peninsula Hotel, and then up to the rooftop helipad. I stood there, taking in the view of the city at sunset. There were huge thunderheads building up in the south that I guessed were the typhoon Ricky had mentioned. Soon enough, a chopper appeared in the darkening sky.

Ten minutes later, I was in the backseat next to Nick, looking down on Manila Bay four thousand feet below. We headed north by northwest to Subic Bay. We didn't talk... there was a disconsolate mood, like we were on a special services mission, unlikely to return. It made sense to feel that way after the loss of Ricky and the screw-up on the last mission. There was still a bad taste in my mouth from being set up, and Nick and Dan knew it.

We landed at the Subic Bay helipad and took a waiting car to the Yacht Club. There, with the assistance of two local cops, we made our way onto the upscale marina and found Bodyshot gone. Cursing ourselves for not checking ahead, we returned to the club to speak with the marina operations manager. A chubby little guy with a hairline that receded all the way to the back of his head, he really didn't want to tell us anything. Nick slipped him a note, and he sang like a bird—funny that. He told us Bodyshot had sailed half an hour ago, destined for Hong Kong, and that it was crewed by Vincenzo Cruz and Rommel Torrez. We needed to move fast.

Outside the operations centre, Nick said, "We'll need a fast boat." He sprang into action to organise one.

~ ~ ~

In no time flat, we were aboard Panalo: a beautiful Princess V42 luxury power cruiser moored at the deluxe marina. It belonged to one of Nick's sailing buddies. Nick was licensed to take the helm.

We left the cops at the marina, and the three of us set sail to chase down Bodyshot.

On the flybridge, Nick pushed both throttles full-ahead, and Panalo jumped up on the plane and powered out of Subic Bay.

There was still a streak of orange in the sky from the setting sun. I looked south into the wind and saw dark rolling clouds with intermittent flashes of ominous purple lightning.

I asked anxiously, "Is that a typhoon heading our way?"

"Yes, it goes to show how much Cruz needed to run. No sailor in his right mind would take on the South China Sea with a typhoon like that coming."

"That means we're not in our right minds either," I said, nervously.

"I guess you could say that. It's going to be a rough ride, but this boat can handle it."

I was happy to hear something positive and tried to ignore the imminent threat of the storm. Happy that the boat could handle it, I had my doubts whether I could. I hate boats.

"What's she got under the hood?" I asked.

"Twin 385 p Volvo D6's."

"And the opposition?"

"Bodyshot's a Prima Buccaneer with a Yanmar 500 horse motor. She's faster than us, but with 400 gallons of extra diesel to get her to Hong Kong, she'll be well down on knots."

"How long to run her down?" I queried.

"With a half-hour start on us, probably ninety minutes," Nick replied, seriously hip to all things maritime.

Dan spoke up. "What are we carrying in firepower, Nick?"

"In the cabin bow lock-up, you'll find an M-16 with an M-203 grenade launcher."

"A grenade launcher?" I queried.

"Yeah, it can fire an antipersonnel grenade up to 400 meters," Dan said.

"Jesus, Nick, what are you expecting, a bloody war?" I asked.

"This guy is a cop and probably more heavily armed than us."

Dan went downstairs into the cabin.

"What's a weapon like that doing aboard a recreational boat?"

Nick explained, "All boats that sail the South China Sea and the Philippines are armed to the teeth to protect against pirates, and Panalo is no exception."

"Why is he heading to Hong Kong?" I asked.

"More likely Wai Linig Ding... a smuggler's island between Hong Kong and Macao. I wonder if his partner Ringo Raye knows he's on the run?"

"Should you try radioing him?" I suggested.

"No, not at all. We'd lose the advantage of surprise."

"I think I need a drink," I admitted, feeling the need to calm the fear welling up inside of me. Being in the ocean swell was bad enough for my guts without the thought of facing a sea battle and a typhoon to boot.

"There's a well-stocked bar below... I could do with one myself. Hey, tell Dan to radio Cortez and update him."

"Roger that," I said, heading below.

In the elaborately decorated cabin, I found Dan seated at a table cleaning the M-16.

The cabin was like a plush hotel suite.

"Man, this is pretty fancy."

Dan looked up and grinned at me. "You should see the Jacuzzi up front... there have been some serious parties in here, I'd say," he chuckled.

"Nick said to radio Cortez and give him a heads-up. Want a drink?"

"Never touch the stuff," he growled.

The cellaret was really something, coming close to the ultimate in gimmicked gadgetry and stocked with enough bottles to float a convention. I made the drinks, watching cautiously in case there was another gadget that drank them for you as soon as they were made. The swell was getting rougher by the minute. I struggled up the narrow companionway to the flybridge and handed Nick his drink.

Ten minutes later, after purging my drink, lunch, and breakfast over the side and hoping like hell that was all, I slumped into a chair beside Nick at the helm.

"Nice shade of green you're wearing. It'll get worse if we stop," he said.

"Don't do that! What with the amount of burly I've just dumped over the side, there's probably ten thousand sharks following us," I groaned.

Nick chuckled and then checked the radar.

"There she is, three nautical miles dead ahead."

By now, the sun was low on the horizon.

"Will we catch him before dark?" I asked, worriedly.

"Just."

The answer didn't convince me. The thought of having a battle at night in a two-meter swell that was getting bigger by the second with the approaching typhoon didn't do my seasickness any favours at all. Dan arrived on the bridge dressed like Rambo.

"Holy mackerel, you could be accused of being a weapon of mass destruction," I observed with a pale-faced chuckle.

All of a sudden, Nick backed off the power and said, "I see her!"

CHAPTER NINETEEN

DAN CHECKED OUR heading and said, "Better come at her from the east, we won't be silhouetted by the setting sun."

Nick nodded, made a sharp turn and gunned her. This was shaping up to be our Battle of Trafalgar, and was making me feel very uncomfortable.

After twenty minutes with the sun almost lost on the horizon, Nick swung the boat due west and headed directly for Bodyshot, at ramming speed!

I gripped both sides of the seat white-knuckled as we sped between the rising swell. Each time we hit the swell, on our port side, it picked us up and dumped us off the top at a scary angle. That didn't seem to bother Nick or Dan with their sea legs but it was sure putting streaks in my underpants. To make matters worse, a howling gale had come up and white-topped the swell with a fury.

Nick glanced at the radar.

"Is the typhoon close?" I asked, with tremble in my voice I couldn't disguise.

"Sure is … the worst of it is about an hour away."

I cringed. "This isn't the worst of it? What is it a tsunami? How are we going survive that?"

Before I could get an answer, I was distracted by a zing from a bullet ricocheting off the gunwale right beside me.

"Shit! That was a shot?" I shrieked.

"Get down, they're firing at us!" Dan yelled.

I could hardly hear myself think over the roar of the engine, the gale and the thumping of the boat every time we plummeted off the top of the swell. It was so chaotic, I figured I mightn't even hear the shot that hit me. Times like this makes a mockery of being agnostic and praying to whomever might be listening.

Dan busied himself lining up the M-16 for a shot at them.

Crack! Crack! Crack! His shots set my ears ringing.

"Fit the launcher, Dan!" Nick ordered.

"A grenade?" I queried, thinking it was a bit extreme.

"Can't risk it Axis, they're probably preparing to do the same thing."

I took a sneak peek at Bodyshot — we were about a fifty meters from her mid-ships. I could make-out two men on board and wondered which was Cruz or Rommel. One of them on the bridge silhouetted by the interior light.

"Give Dan some cover," Nick yelled at me. "Aim at those gas tanks on the transom."

"The what?" I almost yelled.

"The stern! Those big blue-painted drums of fuel!" he qualified.

I drew my pistol, rested both elbows on the gunwale, and when Dan moved into his firing position, I emptied the chamber at the target and then ducked down to reload.

Dan braced himself, waited for the boats to level up, and then fired the grenade. It was a top shot — the flybridge of Bodyshot exploded into a massive fireball.

The shockwave from the explosion smacked me in the face. I watched both men on Bodyshot go down. Whoever was at the helm, if he was still alive, would now be dodging a raging fire.

Nick pushed the throttles forward and we sped towards the burning vessel. Just when I thought he was going to ram it, he swung sharply to port, backed the power into reverse and pulled up, right alongside her ... precision boating.

Dan stripped the launcher off the M-16 in a flash and took aim at the stern of Bodyshot expecting the guy there to show from his hiding place.

"When the fire hits those gas tanks she'll blow sky high," Nick warned, loudly.

The storm was hitting hard now ... waves were pounding us and spraying over the bow, both boats were being lifted three or four metres by the swell, and I feared us colliding but I could see Nick was manoeuvring the throttles to keep us apart.

Through the spray, I saw a guy pop up at the stern of Bodyshot and fire a salvo at us. We ducked. I heard a clunk beside me ... looked down. It was Dan. He was on the deck grasping a badly bleeding shoulder. Nick pulled the M-16 out of his hands, took aim, and let go a barrage of shots at the shooter. I covered the flybridge.

I saw him go down. "You hit him!" I yelled.

Nick stopped firing.

"If you want the evidence ... you'll need to board her."

"What do you mean you Kemosabe?" I complained. "You've got to be kidding!" I yelled to get over the mayhem while staring wide-eyed at the yawing boats.

"Unless you want to take the helm so I can do it!" Nick said, doubtingly.

There was no way. Dan was down, Nick needed to be at the helm — the rest was up to me.

A huge wave splashed over our bow. Nick struggled to keep his feet with the force of it. Soaked to the skin, he yelled at me, "I'll get us up close for you to jump."

Gale force winds, an impossible sea — I watched Bodyshot rising up high and then plummeting down in the massive swell — how on earth was I going to time a jump like that? I handed Nick my smartphone — put the .38 down the back of my pants — then, totally lacking in confidence, I set myself to leap aboard a boat that was yawing in the swell, ablaze, and expected to explode at any moment with two murdering maniacs on board. Who says I get paid enough? I groaned to myself.

"Jump when I yell go," Nick hollered.

I climbed up and balanced myself on the gunwale with my heart in my throat and my knees trembling, transfixed on the burning boat rising and falling in the monstrous swell. The spray from the waves crashing over our bow was hitting me in the face and stinging my eyes. We rose to the top of the swell — I glared down at Bodyshot three metre below us. All hell was breaking loose.

Nick screamed out, "Go!"

I shut my eyes and leapt into my destiny. I was thrilled when both feet hit the deck of Bodyshot together. In overdrive, I rushed towards the burning cabin. To get there I needed to step over a body. It was gory … he was on his back … the bullet had taken out his eye and on exit blown the back of his head clean off. There was blood, bone and brain matter everywhere. The fire wasn't as bad as I first thought, but diesel was spewing from holes in the drums forming into a puddle on the deck and that was certainly something to worry about.

I'd made up my mind to brave a run to the cabin, when suddenly someone appeared in front of me silhouetted by the flames of the burning bridge. He stepped out onto the companionway with a gun trained on me. My Converse trainers slipped in the pool of blood and I nearly slipped over. I raised my pistol. It was a Mexican standoff.

"Give up Cruz or we'll both go up in flames," I yelled.

"How do you know my name, Stone?"

"Same way you know mine, now drop it!"

By the look on his face my order didn't impress him. I presumed he was at his wits end and prepared to go down with the ship. Trouble was, he was determined to take me with him. Well, not this little black duck. I needed to distract him.

"Who killed Chiki Dee?"

"Who cares?" he barked.

"You should, because they'll pin her murder on you along with the hit on Ricky Esposo and the murder of Pablo Cortez!"

"Like I said ... who cares? Bad luck about Esposo ... I've had enough talking to..."

Before he could mutter another word a burst of gunfire caused blood to spray from half a dozen holes in his chest. He contorted like a puppet on a string. I hit the deck to avoid the shot he got away as his knees buckled and he collapsed on the deck a bloody mess.

Nick screamed out, "Go! Damn it! Go!"

I struggled to my feet and hurried through the billowing smoke into the cabin. It was difficult to see in the thick haze. I swiftly removed my T-shirt and used it as a makeshift filter for the fumes. Like a blind man, I extended my arm and felt my way through the cabin towards the forward toilet. When my hand encountered the wall, I groped for the door handle and gripped it firmly. With a click, the door swung open—I located the light switch and flicked it on. The illumination revealed a diminished amount of smoke in the forward sleeper. The toilet was situated on the port side. I could sense the heat emanating from the inferno in the flybridge above—it was only a matter of minutes before the floor would give way to the flames. I opened the small door, switched on the light, lifted the wooden toilet seat, and discovered a wad of chewing gum adhered to the underside, just as Kitty had described. I instinctively reached for my phone to take some photos, but then recalled that I had given it to Nick. Instead, I forcefully tore off the toilet seat to preserve it as evidence.

A deafening whump jolted the boat violently, sending me sprawling to the floor. It seemed like a gas tank had exploded. Through the flapping door, battered by the erratic motion of the boat, I caught sight of flames devouring the main cabin, confirming my fears. Struggling to my feet, I positioned my head through the toilet seat, stowed my gun back in my pants, and doused myself with water from the washbasin tap. To survive, I would have to navigate the raging flames with incredible speed.

I darted into the black smoke, the scorching flames licking and singeing my body. Holding my breath, I raced up the stairs onto the blazing deck. The thought struck me that the remaining tanks were on the verge of exploding. Without sparing a glance for Nick or Panalo, I leaped onto the gunwale and plunged into the water. It felt as if I were suspended in mid-air for an eternity, until a mighty explosion propelled me even further into the void. With a colossal splash, I resurfaced just in time to witness Bodyshot succumbing to the depths. As I cursed Nick for leaving me behind, a lifebuoy landed beside me in the water. Fearing a lurking shark eyeing my vulnerable legs, I seized the lifebuoy with urgency, and to my immense relief, I was promptly hoisted aboard Panalo.

Nick derived great amusement from seeing me emerge from the water, resembling a drowned rat with my head still encased in the toilet seat. However, I was far from amused... shivering uncontrollably, more from shock than from the cold. At least we had acquired the crucial evidence we needed—Bodyshot had met its demise, taking kidnappers Cruz and Rommel down with it.

Dan required immediate medical attention. I knelt down beside him, unbuttoned his shirt, and tore a strip from it to fashion a makeshift bandage to stem the bleeding—it proved effective, ensuring his survival. However, I remained uncertain about my own fate during the treacherous two-hour journey through the relentless typhoon and biblical-sized waves back to Subic Bay. I held little hope of keeping down whatever remained in my gut.

~ ~ ~

By the time we moored at the Yacht Club marina, it felt like I had thrown up every meal I had ever had—I was feeling awful. The boat had hardly come to a stop when I jumped off the thing, fell on my knees in the pouring rain, and kissed the wharf, swearing I would never set foot on anything that floats again.

Nick had radioed ahead for paramedics to attend to Dan. He had also arranged for a local replacement chopper pilot. However, with the typhoon still relentlessly pounding, it would be at least another hour before we could take to the air. The winds were so fierce that they whipped the torrential rain, stinging my face and making it difficult to walk.

We purchased a change of clothes from a club shop and then settled in the café to wait for the storm to subside. Nick handed back my smartphone that I had given him on the boat.

"Here, you know we'll need to be even more cautious now," Nick said solemnly. "We may have just sprung a trap on Raye, but we both know it won't end there... not by a long shot."

"I hear you," I replied. "You must be thinking Sancho failed to arrest him."

Nick raised a sceptical eyebrow. "You read my mind."

I checked my phone, but I couldn't make a call— the typhoon had robbed me of a signal.

"What about this Mayor Rodriguez? It seems guys like him need to face justice even more than the likes of Raye," I pondered.

Nick nodded in agreement. "They call it the Judas Belt."

"Explain," I requested.

"In the Philippines, a Judas Belt is a firecracker—a string of firecrackers, in fact, starting from a small one that goes all the way up to one big mother of a banger at the end."

"Oh, I get it. Corruption starts small but goes all the way to the top," I deduced.

"Exactly, and Mayor Rodriguez sits right on top. He has the ear of the President and considers himself above the law," Nick explained.

"So, even if we apprehend Raye and he blows the whistle on Rodriguez, no one will hear it?" I said.

"Look, the system of corruption runs so deep here that it would take decades for someone to fix it, and they would be risking their life. Every presidential candidate swears they will fix it to get elected, but as soon as they take office, they buy into it," Nick revealed.

It made sense. It was the same back home, albeit less overt. "So, Rodriguez will simply continue his actions even though he is as guilty as Cruz and Raye?"

"Yes, his political position shields him from suspicion," Nick confirmed.

I gazed despondently at the storm outside, lashing Subic Bay, and the eerie silence that the large glass clubhouse windows provided—it felt like a metaphor. "That's completely wrong," I exclaimed.

CHAPTER TWENTY

NICK SAID THE typhoon had passed and it was safe to fly. After the ordeal he had gotten us through on the South China Sea, I wasn't about to doubt him. Within the hour, we were in the air, headed for Makati. It was a bumpy ride, probably due to the dirty air left by the typhoon, and I wasn't entirely comfortable with the new pilot. I don't like pilots or bus drivers who wear a worried expression—it doesn't inspire confidence. Nonetheless, he managed to get us there in one piece. Before parting ways on the roof of the Peninsula, Nick and I agreed to meet in my hotel room the next day at 2 P.M.

~ ~ ~

Feeling fragile, I entered my hotel room and found Lola sound asleep in bed.

It was midday before we finally got out of the sack. Lola ordered breakfast, and soon enough, I was recharged with renewed energy, ready to take on the world again... as long as it had nothing to do with a boat. I filled Lola in on what had happened on the high seas, and as I listened to myself recounting the story, it sounded like a scene from a James Bond movie. Lola sat there, eyes wide as dinner plates, mouth agape, completely shocked and horrified. I may have embellished a few details for added impact, but we can chalk that up to poetic license.

~ ~ ~

Nick and Sancho arrived on time, but Sancho brought bad news. It was exactly what Nick and I had anticipated—his task force had raided Ringo's apartment to make an arrest, but it seemed Ringo had other plans and was nowhere to be found.

"This presents us with an extreme problem," Sancho warned. "No-one is safe with this criminal on the loose."

"I don't understand," Lola said, frowning. "With Cruz dead and Kitty safe, why is Raye still a threat?"

"Because he has lost everything," Nick explained warmly.

I added, "We believe Raye is the mastermind behind this whole operation, and he's terrified that Kitty will expose him."

"God, then we should get her back to Brisbane where it's safe," Lola gasped.

"No, Miss Lovejoy, that's too dangerous... this is the same man who had Ricky targeted in broad daylight, that's how dangerous he is!" Sancho warned firmly.

"Sancho, have you received any updates from the mayor's office since you reopened the case?" I inquired.

"Yes, I called them this morning to report on the hit on Ricky and what happened on board Bodyshot."

"And?" I pressed for more information.

"I was given the green light to arrest Raye on suspicion of conspiracy to kidnap."

"Does that mean we're in the clear as far as Rodriguez is concerned?" I questioned.

"I wouldn't think so," Nick replied. "What we've done has put him in a position where he needs to make Raye his sacrificial lamb."

"I can't believe Rodriguez is going to get away with this," I groaned.

"Oh, I think once it's all over, there may be supporters of Raye who seek to settle the score with Mayor Rodriguez," Sancho said, a wry smile forming on his face, which Nick mirrored.

This time, I got the hint Rodriguez might have a hefty price to pay for his corruption. However, we still needed a plan to capture Raye, and suddenly an idea struck me. It took some convincing, but by the end of the meeting, we had agreed upon a strategy.

~ ~ ~

Later, Lola and I went for dinner at a Japanese restaurant in the mall opposite the Shangri-La. We returned to the Shang around 10 P.M. and were heading to the lobby bar for a nightcap when The Terrible Tango ringtone alerted an incoming text message. It was from Ringo, who wanted to meet me urgently at his club, Foxy's—alone.

"What is that ringtone of yours?" Lola asked.

"Oh, The Terrible Tango, a favourite song by a friend of mine."

"I see, so who was that then?"

"Our friend Ringo Raye. He wants to meet me at his club tonight."

"Tonight! You're not thinking of going, are you? He'll kill you."

"Yes, I am."

"Are you crazy!" she screamed venomously, just subdued enough to avoid causing a scene in the lobby.

"Shhh," I tried to quiet her down and took her by the elbow, leading her to a seat. She angrily pulled away before we reached it and stood glaring at me, arms folded defiantly, and tapping her foot restlessly on the floor. I recognised the body language—I was never going to win, so I resorted to pleading.

"Look Lola, there are things I have to do regarding your and Kitty's safety that come with the gig. You need to trust me. It's why you hired me, right?"

"Like what, trust you to get yourself killed?" she snapped.

Now we were drawing attention, and I could feel the prying eyes of other guests.

"Let's go up to the room and talk about it there," I suggested.

Surprisingly, she agreed, so we took the elevator to our floor, with her giving me the cold shoulder the whole way. I led her into the room, tossed the keycard onto the coffee table, and slumped into a chair with a sense of defeat.

"At least call Nick or Sancho and let them know what you're thinking of doing," she said, venom dripping from her words.

"He told me to come alone, Lola. If I call Sancho, it could turn into a shootout. If Nick comes, anything could happen and put both of us at risk. Do you want that?"

"Are you trying to be a hero or something?" she snarled.

I wasn't accustomed to her wrath. "No way! Look, I'm just trying to do what I believe is necessary. If I don't show up, he'll know something's wrong, and that will ruin our plan."

"And if he decides to hold you hostage for Kitty?" she retorted bitterly.

"That's unlikely to happen," I reassured her.

"What the hell does he want to talk to you about anyway?" she argued.

"I'm not sure, but probably a deal. I'll only find out if I see him. He's backed into a corner...running out of options. I'm his only contact. By now, he knows Cruz is dead and we're closing in on him. If I were in his shoes, I'd try to cut a deal."

"You're delusional. The guy is a gangster."

She flopped onto the sofa and nervously chewed on a fingernail. "If he kills you, I'll never speak to you again," she groaned with a sardonic grimace.

~ ~ ~

I hopped a cab and in no time flat, I found myself in front of Foxy's nightclub. However, when I mentioned Raye's name, the imposing doorman pointed me further down Kalayaan Avenue to another club. I made my way to the entrance of the Blue Velvet Club, reminded of the David Lynch movie and hoping I wouldn't encounter a twisted clown singing Roy Orbison's 'In Dreams' inside.

The club was small, lacking a doorman, and showed little signs of activity. Only the thumping bass from the disco music upstairs hinted that it was open. I climbed a poorly lit staircase that led to the second-floor club. I had chosen to leave my trusty pistol behind in the hotel room, believing it would be best not to bring it along. Sometimes being unarmed avoids escalating situations.

At the top of the stairs, I pushed aside a blue velvet curtain and entered the club. I paused inside to case the joint. There were two main rooms. The larger one was dimly lit, with small alcoves for privacy and a tiny circular dance floor in the centre, adorned with a floor-to-ceiling chrome pole. The adjacent room featured a well-lit pool table, where two foreigners were engaged in a game of nine-ball. Next to it, a bar stretched along the back wall. A Filipina bartender, dressed in a revealing leather dominatrix outfit, served behind the bar. Three bikini-clad girls sat at the bar. The club's decor resembled Patricia Norris' production design storyboard for Blue Velvet. Just as I took a vacant stool and positioned myself with my back to the bar, the song changed to Bed of Roses. At that moment, a stunning Filipina, dressed in a dark blue string bikini with long black hair cascading down to the back of her knees, stepped onto a small stage and gracefully took hold of the chrome pole. Bathed in a single spotlight, she began an enticing pole dance that made me appreciate the Bon Jovi song in a whole new light.

The closest of the three girls sitting beside me, who had been keeping her eyes fixed on me since I sat down, gracefully rose from her seat and approached me as if we were long-lost lovers. With a mischievous smirk on her heavily painted face, she whispered in my ear, requesting a drink. I swivelled around, called the bartender over, and ordered her a glass of her preferred drink, along with a JD for myself. I was just starting to immerse myself in Manila's nightlife when the lights suddenly went out.

~ ~ ~

When I opened my eyes, black spots were performing a kind of shimmering dance that then faded away to some place in the wings. There was no applause. As the haze cleared, the snarling face of Arnel Gutierrez came into focus.

"Welcome to Blue Velvet, Stone," he sneered, waving his gun around as if it were a toy. "You bragged about having a better skill-set, didn't you?"

"How come Raye sends a boy to do a man's work?" I glanced down at the rope that bound me, hogtied in the chair. Surrounded by darkness, with only the illumination from an overhead spotlight, I knew I must be in the back room of the club. Bon Jovi's Bed of Roses was coming to an end, so I estimated I had only been out for a minute or so.

Gutierrez signalled someone in the darkness, and a large bruiser materialised like an apparition. I recognised him as the hulking doorman from Foxy's. He delivered an open-handed slap across my face, stinging and rattling my senses.

Shaking my head, I retorted, "If that's your way of saying hello, I'll be avoiding you in the future, pal. What do you want, Gutierrez? You're just a coward who resorts to attacking from behind. Untie me, and we can settle this between us." I managed to speak through clenched teeth, tasting blood from my split lip. Fatso had done a number on me, and he prepared for a second blow, but Gutierrez intervened.

"Shut up! I want Kitty, and guess what, buddy? You're going to deliver her to me."

"Don't be ridiculous. She's not in any condition to travel," I responded.

"That's exactly how I want her. Cut the bullshit, Stone... It'll only get your dumbass face messed up more than it is already," Gutierrez snarled.

"You're tough when you have a gun and Fatso here to do your dirty work," I growled. "Where's Ringo? I answered his call to talk, not yours!"

"Either play it my way, or I'll leave you in the street with your wrists slit," Gutierrez threatened.

On cue, Fatso pulled out a switchblade and flicked it open. The message was clear. I got the hint.

"Okay, okay, you win this round. So, how do you want to play this?" I relented.

"You deliver Kitty to me, then leave the Philippines... If you don't, you'll be extending your stay in the city morgue. Got it?"

"What makes you think I have that kind of influence? I'm just hired help, like you," I retorted.

My response earned me another slap across the face, this time from Gutierrez himself. I moved with the blow, lessening the impact. Why do I always have to be a smartass in these situations? Maybe I'm a masochist.

"I don't give a crap how you do it, Stone," Gutierrez spat. "Just make it happen."

"Look, you can work me over all you like but it's not going to get you anywhere."

That really pissed Gutierrez off. He opened his .38, emptied out all but one shell, revolved the chamber, shut it with a click and then put the barrel up to my right eye.

"You thin your life means anything to me, Stone?"

"I hope not. Your life certainly means nothing to me," I shot back.

He pulled the trigger, and I winced at the loud click from the empty chamber. My heart was pounding in my throat, but I needed to maintain my composure.

"I win," I stated, a smug grin on my face.

"Want to go another round, tough guy?" Gutierrez threatened, pressing the gun into my eye.

"Alright, alright... That's enough, or you'll give me myopia," I complained.

"Agree to hand her over, or the next time, you'll be with your friends Vargas and Cortez it'll be at your funeral. Do I make myself clear?"

"If I hand her over to you, then what? You'll kill her? Are you asking me to sign Kitty's death warrant?" I challenged.

"No-one said anything about killing her," Gutierrez replied.

"Then why go to all this trouble?" I pressed.

"We just need a little time with her to straighten out some personal problems," he explained.

"A Zoom call could accomplish that," I quipped.

"That's not up to me, Stone! Just agree, damn it. I'm running out of patience here," Gutierrez demanded. He nodded at Fatso, and the large man emerged from the darkness, delivering a powerful slap to the side of my head. My right ear rang as if I had just attended a Metallica concert. He followed it up with a heavy punch to my gut, leaving me doubled over and gasping for air.

Gutierrez growled, "You leave me no choice, Stone."

He muttered something in Tagalog to Fatso, who grabbed at my pants belt, unfastened it, and yanked my pants down to my knees. He then melted back into the darkness, and Gutierrez reappeared.

"I hate to do this to a virile man like you, but you leave me no choice. Nut him!" he ordered.

I caught a glimmer of light reflecting off the switchblade Fatso produced on cue, and I realised Gutierrez intended to end my sex life prematurely. Fatso pulled down the front of my underpants, took hold of my manhood, and positioned the blade ready to chop the lot.

"Hey, hold it right there!" I appealed. "You've convinced me. I have no desire to join the Vienna Boys Choir."

"Sorry, but I'm not convinced you're convinced, Stone. You can still be of value to me, even without your family jewels. It's important to make an example out of you," Gutierrez sneered.

"No, no, it isn't. In fact, it's completely unnecessary... I'll do what you want. Just order Fatso to let go of my tackle and back off," I pleaded.

Fatso released his grip, and I breathed a sigh of relief. However, another nod from Gutierrez prompted Fatso to grab my testicles again, squeezing them so tightly that it felt like they were about to burst. The pain was excruciating, and I blacked out.

CHAPTER TWENTY-ONE

I **WOKE UP** in a filthy, foul-smelling alley, surrounded by rats and garbage. To my horror, I realised I was lying on a bed of rubbish that included used syringes. I cursed Gutierrez, but it didn't change my situation. Escaping this hazardous mess without getting pricked by an infected needle would require some effort. The memory of Bed of Roses playing in Blue Velvet crossed my mind, and I wondered if this was some sick joke orchestrated by Gutierrez.

I heard a noise, followed by chuckling and the sound of running water. Someone was relieving themselves in the alley. I called out for help.

"Hey, can you lend me a hand?"

Two faces appeared over me. I recognised them as the two men who had been playing pool at Blue Velvet earlier. They were both foreigners and clearly intoxicated.

The taller man spoke with a Scottish accent, "Hey mate, looks like you've had a few too many."

Deciding to play along, I slurred my words, pretending to be drunk. "Can hardly move, mate," I mumbled. "What's that smell?"

"You're lying in a pile of shite, mate," the smaller man with an Irish accent replied. "Jesus, will you look at all those syringes he's laid on! For God's sake fella, don't move, you don't know what's in those things!" he exclaimed worriedly.

They lifted me up, being careful not to disturb the pile of trash, and propped me against the alley wall. I let myself slide down as if I couldn't stand upright.

"You better sleep it off right there, mate," the Irishman advised. "Come on Gordy, let's get a move on."

Pretending to doze off, I listened as their laughter faded into the night. Once I was sure they were gone, I struggled to my feet. The sight of the bed of syringes and filth I had been rescued from sent shivers down my spine. I was grateful I hadn't woken up and tried to free myself, risking a needle prick. I stumbled out of the alley, finding myself on Kalayaan Street. The Blue Velvet club was just a few doors down, and I knew the Shangri-La was a decent walk away. I didn't feel like taking a cab, so I decided to walk.

As I made my way toward Foxy's, I half-hoped to encounter Fatso at the door so I could give him a taste of his own medicine. But self-preservation prevailed, and I crossed the road to avoid his menacing switchblade.

P. Burgos Street was lined with small nightclubs boasting exotic names like Ivory, the Mascara Bar, and Jools. The larger clubs had spruikers at the entrance, luring customers in for expensive drinks, a show, and perhaps a bit of slap and tickle.

My watch showed it was 4 A.M., which meant most bars on the strip were closing. The pavement was congested with foreigners vying for the few available taxis. I was glad I had chosen to walk to the Shang.

I crossed P. Burgos Street near its junction with Makati Avenue, knowing that it led all the way to the Shangri-La. The sun was beginning to rise by the time I finally reached my hotel room. Quietly entering, careful not to wake Lola, I was too exhausted to take a shower. I climbed into bed beside her. Just as I was drifting off into a well-deserved sleep, I heard her voice groaning in the distance.

"Hi, when did you get in? Are you alright?"

"Just now," I croaked. "Sorry to wake you."

I rolled onto my side, wrapped my arm around her, and crashed.

I woke up to the sound of the shower running. Squinting at the bedside clock, I realised it was already eleven forty. I desperately needed a bath to wash away the stench of rubbish. With great effort, I managed to get out of bed and tagged lovely Lola to hop in the shower. While I freshened up, Lola ordered breakfast for us.

Once we had satisfied our hunger, I settled into a comfortable lounge chair, sipping a steaming cup of coffee. I couldn't help but admire Lola, dressed in a stunning purple dress. Her blonde hair was elegantly styled, emphasizing her beautifully sculpted neck, and her long, smooth legs were crossed in front of her. Her open high-heeled sandals showcased her perfectly pedicured feet.

"Do my feet turn you on?" she teased, a mischievous smile on her face.

"Every inch of you turns me on, Lola, but when it comes to your feet, let's just say they hold a special appeal for a man with a serious foot fetish," I replied playfully.

Just then, the house phone rang, interrupting the moment. I got up and answered it.

"Hello, yes... put him on... Hi Nick. Agreed, yeah, had a little run-in with them last night. No Arnel Gutierrez and a henchman. Yeah, I'll fill you in when I get there."

I hung up and returned to my seat. Lola had been to the bathroom while I was on the phone and re-joined me.

"I'm going to meet Nick at the Manila Yacht Club," I informed her.

"What about Arnel?" she asked, a hint of concern in her voice.

"If he wants Kitty, then he can have her," I replied.

"What?" she screamed in disbelief. "I can't believe you just said that!"

"Wait, wait... we have a plan. Just calm down," I reassured her.

It had come to this point, and now the biggest challenge would be convincing Lola to trust in our scheme.

~ ~ ~

As I stepped out onto the street, the oppressive humidity enveloped me like a suffocating wet blanket. I quickly hailed a cab to take me to the Manila Yacht Club. I had agreed to text Gutierrez the location for him to collect Kitty, but I had no intention of blindly following his instructions. He must have been delusional to think I would play along without question. Nonetheless, I didn't want to raise any suspicions, so I decided to stick to the plan. On the way, I called Cortez to bring him up to speed. The traffic was incredibly congested, and the short distance took nearly an hour to traverse. I couldn't help but think that I could have walked faster.

Finally, the cab dropped me off in front of the club. As I approached the entrance, an uneasy feeling washed over me, as if I were being watched. I scanned the car park but didn't spot Nick's black Pajero, indicating that he hadn't arrived yet.

CHAPTER TWENTY-TWO

I ENTERED THE Manila Yacht Club after dropping the name of Vargas at the reception. The staff immediately escorted me to a table where a refreshing Wallbanger cocktail awaited me. I settled into a plush leather armchair, taking in the breathtaking view of Manila Bay. As my mind wandered, envisioning the historical battles that once took place in these waters, Nick joined me at the table.

"A penny for your thoughts?" he sighed.

"I was looking at the bay and imagining the American armada anchored off Corregidor bombarding the area," I replied.

"Over a million Filipinos lost their lives in that battle," Nick remarked.

We raised our glasses in a toast to Ricky and Chiki, our fallen comrades, before taking a sip of our drinks.

"Tell me about last night," Nick urged.

"I got a message to meet Raye at his club, Foxy's," I explained.

"And you went alone? Man, do you have a death wish?" Nick exclaimed.

"I hear you, but he specifically instructed me to come alone. What can I say, it's my job," I replied.

"I suppose it was a trap," Nick mused.

"Exactly as we expected. Arnel Gutierrez and his goon ambushed me. They wanted me to agree to hand over Kitty. It was inevitable," I admitted.

"He chose Gutierrez instead of appearing himself. We were prepared for either scenario," Ricky chimed in.

"How many goons do you think Raye has?" I asked.

"With a high-profile criminal like him, it's hard to say. In times of desperation, he could call in favours and assemble quite a force," Nick replied.

"He might have a small army at his disposal," I contemplated.

"Yes, but it's unlikely. What's troubling you, Axis?" Nick inquired.

"This Gutierrez guy is unpredictable. Let me tell you, one wrong answer last night, and I would be lying on a slab at the morgue. I don't mind dealing with Raye, but Gutierrez is a different story … a loose cannon."

Finishing our drinks, we left the club and headed to the car park.

"How's Dan?" I asked.

Nick nodded, "He'll be fine, one tough hombre."

"We could sure use him now."

As we walked, I couldn't shake off the feeling of being watched. I noticed a suspicious vehicle with two occupants observing us.

"I think we have company," I informed Nick.

We got into the Pajero. Nick glanced at his side mirror and confirmed, "Yeah, I saw them when I arrived. Looks like they followed you. Did you text Gutierrez?"

"Yep, and he replied," I assured him.

"Good. Let's take our friends on a little ride, shall we?" Nick suggested.

Starting the engine, we navigated through the congested traffic of Roxas Boulevard. The ten-minute trip turned into a thirty-minute ordeal. Finally, we arrived at Asian Terminals, the Vargas family business. Being a Sunday, it was closed. Nick used a remote to open the large gates, and we passed through, coming to a stop on the other side.

I kept an eye on the car that had been tailing us as we waited. Nick made a call, speaking in Tagalog, and confirmed the plan was in motion. Suddenly, he looked alarmed.

"We have more company," he informed me.

I turned around and saw another car pulling up beside the one that had followed us.

"The more, the merrier," I nervously quipped, aware that everything hinged on our plan succeeding.

"They're here," Nick announced.

Checking behind us, I saw an ambulance approaching the entrance. I patted Nick's knee, offering him good luck.

We shook hands, and I opened the door, stepping out of the Pajero and awaiting the arrival of the ambulance. As it stopped inside the gates, a paramedic emerged, opening the back hatch and lowering a ramp. Another medic wheeled Kitty down the ramp in a wheelchair. Once she was out, the paramedics closed the hatch, got back into the ambulance, executed a U-turn, and drove away, leaving Kitty with me. I positioned her wheelchair to face the gates and waited.

Our unwanted guests stepped out of their vehicles. Two of them approached us, while the remaining two, armed with handguns, kept a watchful eye. I recognised Fatso among them. As the two individuals approached, I realised one of them was Arnel.

The ambulance stopped just beyond the two cars.

"Here to handle your own dirty work for once, Ringo?" I sarcastically remarked.

"Only to collect my property. How are you, Kitty?" Ringo retorted.

Kitty, sitting in the wheelchair with her head down and wearing a black hat, slowly raised her head and locked eyes with him.

"Hello, Ringo," she sneered, her top lip curling maliciously. "So, Arnel, are you going to shoot me right here, just like you did with Pablo?"

"That's not my call," Arnel snapped.

"No, Kitty, that's not what will happen here," Ringo declared forcefully. "You're coming with me."

"The hell I am!" she shrieked, surprising them both. She pulled a gun out from under the blanket and aimed it at Arnel. Before he could react, she fired, hitting him in the shoulder. Arnel went down.

Nick jumped out of the Pajero with an M-16, propped himself up on the bonnet, and aimed at Ringo. "One move out of you or your men, Raye, and you're dead!" he yelled.

Ringo immediately raised his hands, and his men lowered their guns as Cortez and three other cops stormed out of the back of the ambulance, taking Raye's men at gunpoint. Kitty covered me while I patted Raye down and took his gun. The situation was under control.

Nick approached Ringo, keeping the M-16 trained on him. "On the ground with your hands behind your head, Raye," he ordered firmly.

Raye complied and turned his head on the ground, glaring at Kitty. "You've committed suicide, Kitty," he growled, bristling with anger.

"I've got no idea what you're talking about, Ringo," she replied calmly.

"I'll credit you, I didn't think you had the guts, but it's still suicide," he spat angrily.

"My suicide blonde," I fired back at him.

"Blonde, ha! Not Kitty, shows how much you know, Stone!" he mocked.

"You're probably right, Kitty might not have the guts, but her sister Lola certainly does!" I laughed.

Lola stepped out of the wheelchair, removed her hat, and let her long golden locks fall onto her shoulders. Ringo looked up, completely astounded. His ego was shattered—defeated by a woman.

"You're not Kitty!" he exclaimed, his whole body shaking with rage.

Cortez took great pride in personally slapping the cuffs on Ringo. Finally, he had his nemesis in custody. He cuffed Arnel, his brother's killer.

Police cars arrived to remove the prisoners. I gave Lola a big hug. "You're a brave suicide blonde," I said.

"Yeah, but a lousy shot," she replied with a chuckle.

"Why's that?" I asked, joining in the laughter.

"I was aiming at his head!"

Nick approached us with the M-16 resting on his shoulder, looking like a mercenary on the front cover of Time Magazine. "Glad that's finally over. Well done, Lola. Your sister would be proud of you."

"Speaking of Kitty, where is she?" I asked Nick.

"She's on my boat. Let's go there now?"

"No way, man! I'm allergic to boats," I joked.

We laughed together. Cortez joined us and singled me out. "Thank you, amigo," he said with a big gold tooth grin. We shook hands.

"We wouldn't have pulled it off without Lola's brilliant deception," I said.

"That took a lot of nerve, Lola. Your family can rest assured these criminals will pay dearly for their crimes," Cortez commended.

"Thank you, inspector," Lola replied with a smile.

I took great joy in watching both Arnel and Fatso being herded handcuffed into the back seat of a police vehicle. I couldn't resist giving Arnel a final taunt. "There will be a Bed of Roses waiting for you in prison. Now, who's got the best skill-set? Huh! And you, Fatso, maybe you can share the bed of roses with him."

They growled in frustration, but they knew I had the last laugh.

~ ~ ~

I sipped on my feral Harvey Wallbanger at the Manila Yacht Club, the familiar taste tingling my taste buds. Lola sat across from me, and I couldn't help but smile at her. "Happy days, kiddo," I said, raising my glass in a toast.

Lola returned the smile but sighed softly. "It's a shame we can't stay a little longer to enjoy Manila."

My gaze turned mischievous as I leaned forward. "If we stayed, we might not leave the bedroom," I teased, an evil glint in my eye.

Just as I reached out to take Lola's hand, Nick and Kitty arrived, drawing my attention. Standing up, I greeted them with enthusiasm.

"Look at you, Kitty! Able to walk and looking like a complete sex kitten!" I exclaimed, pulling Kitty into a warm hug.

Kitty kissed her sister and settled down beside her. As we all took our seats, I couldn't help but notice the contrast between Lola and Kitty. Lola exuded warmth and openness, while Kitty had a hint of aloofness, perhaps a remnant of her past in the seedy world of nightclubs and criminals.

Curiosity got the better of me, and I turned to Kitty. "So, what happens from here, Kitty?"

Kitty let out a sigh, her eyes filled with mixed emotions. "I don't know, really. Dad wants me back in Brisbane, but I still crave the high-life. I can't see myself wasting away on the Gold Coast, singing in casino piano bars and pubs."

Lola interjected wisely, "Hey sis, look where the high-life got you this time."

Nick added, "It nearly got all of us killed."

I couldn't help but feel a pang of sadness. "It certainly ended the lives of Ricky Esposo and Chiki Dee preterm."

"Yeah, well, when you put it like that...I... I..." Kitty's voice trailed off, tears welling up in her eyes.

Nick placed a comforting arm around her, trying to lighten the mood. "Hey, how about we go to Australia? Take a few weeks, and you can show me all the sights. After that, we can figure out what's next."

Amidst the tears, a glimmer of hope emerged in Kitty's eyes. Perhaps having Nick by her side could be the remedy she needed.

Nick chuckled and added, "Hard to believe a lump of chewing gum cracked the case for us."

Laughter filled the air as we all joined in, finding solace in the absurdity of the situation.

As the laughter subsided, Lola turned to me with a smug expression on her face, wiping away her tears. "What about you, private investigator Axis Stone? Any more thrilling cases waiting for you?"

I feigned nonchalance, attempting to conceal the truth. "Oh, you know me, Lola. Cases are piling up. I'll probably head back to old Sydney town soon, provided I've been paid, of course."

Just then, a hand descended from above, placing a Harvey Wallbanger in front of me. To my surprise, it lacked the usual tropical foliage garnish. I looked up at the waiter, astonishment evident on my face.

"What happened to the foliage?" I inquired.

The waiter smiled, understanding my preference. "We got the hint that you prefer it without, sir."

Nick chimed in, grinning from ear to ear. "You see, my friend, we might appear to be a bit backward, but we eventually catch on."

"There's hope for you lot yet," I said, raising my glass in a toast. "Here's looking at you."

Lola turned to Nick, her voice tinged with longing. "Nick, do you think it's safe for me to stay a few more days with Kitty?"

Nick reassured her, "Absolutely. You're both welcome to stay with me. Until we lock up Raye and throw away the key, none of us are safe. We can even take a sail to the islands for a week or two while we're at it. Kitty will likely be required in court by then."

I turned to Kitty, curiosity piqued once again. "That reminds me, what do you have on Raye that made him want to silence you?"

Kitty's expression grew serious. "I know about some of his major drug deals, including the one that got Tony Lamont killed. I was present at meetings with his partners, Cruz, and the Gutierrez family."

Lola interjected, seeking clarification. "Who is Tony Lamont?"

"That's the undercover name of Sancho's brother, Pablo Cortez, who was murdered by Arnel Gutierrez," Kitty explained.

Lola turned towards me with a mischievous grin. "You sure we can't persuade you to join us on a leisurely cruise to the islands, Axis?"

I raised an eyebrow, trying to hide my uneasiness. "Very funny, Lola. You should know more than anyone how allergic I am to anything marine."

Undeterred, Lola leaned in and put on a pleading face. "Oh, come on, Axis. Please? It would be so much fun."

Her puppy dog eyes weakened my resolve. "Alright, alright. I'll see what I can do. But I have a couple of things to attend to first."

"Fantastic!" Nick exclaimed. "It's settled, then. We leave in two days. In the meantime, you can all stay at my house, safe from any potential reprisals. So, Axis, what do you need to take care of?"

I took a deep breath, knowing that there were challenges and dangers awaiting me. But with the support of my newfound allies, I was ready to face them head-on.

"I have some loose ends to tie up and a few leads to follow," I replied. "But I'll do my best to wrap things up quickly and join you for the cruise."

With our plans set in motion, we raised our glasses once again, toasting to the future and the adventures that lay ahead.

CHAPTER TWENTY-THREE

I ASKED NICK'S driver to make a stop at an ATM. We pulled into a shopping mall, and I quickly made my way to the automated teller machine. Inserting my card into the slot, I found that the money Winston had promised was indeed there—ten grand. I withdrew four thousand US dollars, stuffed it into my pocket, and returned to the Pajero.

When we arrived at Ricky's parents' home in Diliman, I took out two thousand dollars in cash, equivalent to around a hundred thousand pesos. I placed the money in a Shangri-La envelope, leaving Dom, the driver, in the car. Approaching the front door, I was taken aback when a younger version of Ricky answered. He looked just like his brother.

"You must be Ricky's brother from the States?" I said, slightly surprised. "Boy, you guys look—"

"Yeah, people always say we look like twins. You must be Mr Stone," he interrupted. "I'm William, but my friends call me Billy."

"I came to pay my respects, Billy," I said.

"My parents are at the funeral home. I was just about to catch a jeepney there," Billy replied.

"If you want to direct us, we'll take the Pajero," I offered.

"Hinde problema," he smiled.

Billy had the same mannerisms and personality as Ricky. It was a brief drive until he stopped us outside St. Peters Memorial Chapel in Diliman. Leaving Dom in the car, we entered the chapel complex.

A short walk led us to Mr and Mrs Esposo, seated in a small chapel amidst other mourners. In the centre of the room, on a stand, was an open coffin surrounded by a multitude of wreaths.

As Ricky's mother recognised me, she immediately stood up. I stepped into her warm, sombre embrace, unable to hold back my tears. Ricky's father struggled to his feet and shuffled over to embrace me as well. Their kindness moved me deeply, leaving me speechless.

"I'm so sorry for your loss, Mr and Mrs Esposo," I managed to stammer. "Ricky took a bullet for me, and for that, I will forever be in his debt. I want you to know your son died a hero."

Slipping the envelope into Mr Esposo's trembling hand, I continued, "Please take this. Ricky earned it." It was a lie, but I wanted them to feel a sense of pride and gratitude, not pity.

Billy approached, taking my arm, and led me to the casket. As someone unfamiliar with open coffin viewings and not particularly religious, seeing Ricky's lifeless body laid out like a wax figure at Madame Tussauds unsettled me. Though there was a resemblance, it felt like a mere shell. I went through the motions, bidding my final goodbyes. Billy accompanied me back to the Pajero.

"Dad said there was two thousand dollars in the envelope you gave him," Billy said softly. "Ricky wouldn't have earned that much in six months. It was a kind gesture, and I want to personally thank you, Mr Stone."

"Call me Axis," I said, handing him my business card. "And listen, if you ever want to step into your brother's shoes and become a sleuth, call me. If you're even half as good as Ricky was, you'd be twice as good as anyone else. He was a top bloke, Billy. He took a bullet for me, and nothing I can do or say could ever repay that except to remember him."

We embraced, both of us teary-eyed. It felt as though I had known Billy as well as I did Ricky, and somehow, deep down inside, I knew our paths would cross again somewhere along the dusty dirt track we call life.

~ ~ ~

Dom drove us to the Shangri-La, and he waited outside while I went up to my room to pack. I had been instructed to gather Lola's belongings as well. Upon entering the room, I noticed a blinking message light on the phone. I called the reception and asked them to replay the message for me. It turned out to be a request for a call back from the office of Mayor Rodriguez. However, it was already five thirty, too late to make the call.

I strapped on the side holster and pistol that Ricky had given me for protection. Then, I contacted the concierge and requested assistance with the luggage. Shortly after, a young porter arrived with a trolley to handle the bags. While he took care of the belongings, I made my way to the cashier to check out. As I waited for the bill to be prepared, I noticed a man sitting nearby engrossed in reading the Philippine Star newspaper. The headline on the front page caught my attention: "Ringo Raye arrested on suspicion of murder."

~ ~ ~

By the time we reached Nick's house in Forbes Park, the sun had set. The house was palatial, a mansion boasting a long, winding driveway that led to a four-story structure, snugly nestled amidst beautifully manicured gardens and tropical trees. Dom let me out of the vehicle, then carried the bags inside. My mind was still occupied by the call from the mayor's office; a conversation with Nick was in order.

A maid welcomed me at the front door, guiding me through the vast house to the outdoor swimming pool. There, I found Nick and the Lovejoy sisters savouring a relaxed drink.

"Axis, at last! We had to commence happy hour without you," Nick declared jovially.

I dragged a chair and sank into it, fatigue overtaking me.

"Happy hour," I sighed, "I could use a drink. Nice spread you've got here, mate."

The moment I mentioned a drink, a maid materialised with a tall glass elegantly balanced on a silver tray.

"I hope it's to your liking," Nick remarked, smirking.

I took a sip and announced, "A perfect Wallbanger, brilliant."

"How did you fare with Ricky's family?" Lola inquired.

"I'm not accustomed to the open cask tradition … it just didn't seem like him lying there. It's hard to accept that he was alive and well just a few days ago. Nonetheless, it was good to see his folks and meet his younger brother."

"In line with Filipino tradition, Ricky will be on display for forty days."

"Ew, I don't think I could bear to see someone in that state," Kitty grimaced.

"He resembled a wax dummy," I admitted, wincing.

"The corpse is prepared in such a way that the body can endure the forty days of exposure without decomposing," Nick clarified.

"Doesn't it go off and smell, you know, decompose?" Lola queried, her nose crinkling in distaste.

"No, like Axis pointed out, all that remains is essentially a shell. The organs, bodily fluids, and such are removed and the body is embalmed."

Kitty shivered. "Can we change the subject, please? It's creeping me out."

"When I checked out of the Shangri-La, there was a message to contact the mayor's office. I was too late, so I didn't call. What do you make of that, Nick?"

"Yet another reason we need to leave town pronto," he stated sternly.

"Why? What could possibly happen now?" Lola asked, her expression reflecting her anxiety.

"I suspect he'll want to cut a deal to ensure his complicity doesn't come to light," Nick speculated.

"I saw today's headline in the Philippine Star. It read: 'Ringo Raye accused of murder,'" I shared slowly.

"Interestingly, Nick received a call from a producer at Viva Films an hour ago, asking if they could use his name in a movie," Kitty disclosed, chuckling.

"A movie! About the kidnapping? And everything else that transpired? You must be joking!" I expressed my disbelief.

"I wonder who they'll cast to play me?" Kitty mused, giggling.

"It doesn't take long for them to identify a juicy tale and adapt it into a movie. You can bet they'll produce it while the topic is still trending," Nick added.

"That's absurd," I huffed.

"The worst part is that it will end up as some zany scriptwriter's interpretation of the events, with complete disregard for the actual details," Nick lamented.

"They won't let the truth stand in the way of a good story, right?" I jested.

"Very true," Nick concurred. "It's just another reason why Rodriguez would want to distance himself from it."

"So, what should I do then, Nick?"

"You'd better get in touch with him, Axis, and do it fast," he advised solemnly.

After a fantastic meal, my body crying out for rest, I sluggishly followed Lola and the maid upstairs to our respective bedrooms. The maid left us at the entrance to Lola's room.

"Goodnight, Axis," Lola murmured, pecking me on the cheek. As I basked in a whiff of her perfume, she turned to open the door. I used that moment to admire her splendid figure, starting from her dainty feet barely visible under her long, white satin dress that clung to her like a second skin, up to the plunging neckline that elegantly emphasized her perfect breasts. I sighed in frustration, too exhausted to pursue my desires, and meandered over to my room next door.

"Goodnight, sleep tight," I mumbled.

Upon entering my room and switching on the light, guess who I found? Lola had come in through an adjoining door.

CHAPTER TWENTY-FOUR

I T WAS THE best sleep I'd had in a long while, and waking up next to such an alluring beauty was an indulgence I wished I could experience more often.

The day was once again divine, and having breakfast by the pool in the company of the stunning twins provided a spectacle superior to that offered by the Shangri-La pool brigade.

The Bloody Marys and the brewed coffee were exquisite, and the Eggs Benedict were perhaps the best I'd ever tasted.

"I won't arrange for the chopper to Legazpi City until you've spoken with the Mayor's office," Nick stated. "Tilly," he called, "please bring Mr Stone the phone."

The maid, who was poised to refill our cups with coffee, put the pot down and proceeded to retrieve the phone.

"You're looking better each day, Kitty," I complimented.

Her previously pale face had recovered its colour, and her entire demeanour had improved. She was radiating happiness, the glow of a woman in love.

"Yes, it's amazing what a wonderful man and a good night's sleep can do—better than Botox," she retorted, grinning mischievously.

Tilly returned with a hands-free phone and passed it to me. I checked the number on a piece of paper I had and dialled.

"Yes, hello, I'd like to speak with Mayor Rodriguez, please... My name is Axis Stone, a private detective. Yes, I'll hold."

After a few minutes, the receptionist returned to the line. "Mr Stone, Mayor Rodriguez has asked if you could meet him at the Makati Polo Club at eleven today?"

"One moment, please, while I check," I said, glancing at Nick. "He's asked to meet at the Manila Polo Club at eleven."

"Assure them that it's fine and let them know I'll accompany you. I'm a member," Nick instructed.

~ ~ ~

Dressed in our casual Sunday best, Dom dropped us off at the front door of the grand club, merely a five-minute drive from Nick's house. We stepped into the classical Filipino building, luxuriously enveloped by impeccably trimmed trees and an expansive, meticulously groomed polo field. The interior was a picture of opulence, a testament to old wealth and the grandeur of a bygone era.

"Pretty lavish club, membership must cost an arm and a leg," I remarked.

"I wouldn't know, my family has been members since it was built in the 1950s. There are only two-hundred and thirty-eight lifetime members," Nick replied.

"Would Rodriguez be a lifetime member?"

"No, he's not from old money... nouveau riche. He's probably an associate member."

At the reception, Nick made some inquiries and signed me in as a guest. We then headed to the Sports Café where Mayor Rodriguez awaited us.

The Italian-style café, with its sandstone brick walls and dark red terracotta floor tiles, was relatively empty. Rodriguez stood out like a sore thumb, resembling a Wall Street broker more than a mayor in his evidently expensive black suit. The cunning look on his face and his gargoyle-like henchmen on either side gave me a sense of unease.

"Mr Stone?" he inquired in a deep, accented voice. "And, I presume, Mr Vargas."

177

After exchanging handshakes and sending his guards away with a simple finger flick, Rodriguez offered us a drink.

"It's a bit early for a drink, so a freshly brewed coffee would be fine," I responded.

"I'll second that, thank you," added Nick.

As the waitress scurried to fetch our order, Rodriguez leaned back in his chair, pulled out a plastic dummy cigarette, and started sucking on it, making me glance at the 'No Smoking' sign behind him.

"Well," I began, "you wanted to talk with me?"

"I have some concerns about this case you seem to have handled so proficiently," he started, measuredly. "There may be some resulting issues, so to speak… for one and all, Mr Stone."

"And what would those be, Mayor Rodriguez?" I asked earnestly.

"Well, let's just say that I would like to avoid my name coming up in any way, do you understand?" he said, with a slight nod.

Our coffees arrived. We doctored them with sugar and milk, then waited for the waitress to leave.

I locked eyes with Rodriguez. "No, I can't say that I do understand, Mayor Rodriguez. The only time I've heard your name mentioned in connection with the case was when your office first contacted me after you shut down the police investigation. Unfortunately, I was tied up being shot at and then had to tend to my associate Ricky Esposo, who was busy dying from a drive-by," I said, my words dripping with sarcasm.

"Yes, I heard, most unfortunate," he said, stiffly.

"Two innocent people and an undercover police officer have been murdered, Mayor Rodriguez, and that's why I find it difficult to understand why you'd be worried about your name being involved. If you're innocent, why would you be worried?" I pressed.

"You're not making this any easier for me, Stone."

"Oh, you'll have to pardon me, I seem to have developed an earthly cynicism in the last forty-eight hours," I said.

"This is not a joke, Mr Stone," he said tightly.

Nick chimed in, diplomatically, "Mayor Rodriguez, what Mr Stone means is that we hadn't connected you to the case. Your concerns should lie with Ringo Raye and his associates, not us."

"My concern is with Kitty Lovejoy," he snapped.

Suddenly, I saw through the fog of confusion: Kitty knew that Rodriguez was one of Raye's partners. Nick and I exchanged a knowing glance.

"Let's stop beating around the bush, Mayor Rodriguez. Are you suggesting that Kitty knows something you don't want to be made public?" I asked.

He looked at me blankly for a few seconds, then firmly shook his head. "No, Mr Stone, nothing like that at all."

"You sure?" I croaked.

"Of course," he said. "Let me tell you what is going to happen," he posited smoothly, "Kitty is going to leave for Australia tomorrow vowing never to return to the Philippines. Simple as that," he said. His lips curled into a smirk before he pierced them with his dummy cigarette.

"And in doing so, she will fail to appear in court as the key witness to the prosecution of Ringo Raye and Arnel Gutierrez, correct?" Nick summed up.

"So, they get away with kidnapping and murder?" I added, my tone marked with indignation.

"I'm not in a position to speculate on the outcome of a court case, Mr Stone, nor am I qualified to determine guilt or innocence, Mr Vargas," he replied evenly. "But I trust in the law's ability to deliver justice, regardless of the country. So, gentlemen, do we understand each other?"

"That leaves me with one question, Mayor Rodriguez. What happens if we don't comply?" I probed.

"I'm here merely to suggest an approach in your best interests, Mr Stone. I can't be held responsible for the consequences if you choose to disregard my advice," he responded, his tone flat and emotionless.

Unable to hide my revulsion for the man, I stood up to leave. Taking the cue, Nick stood up as well.

"It's your brand of corruption that holds this country back, Mayor Rodriguez. Goodbye, and thanks for the coffee," I spat, and then stormed out of the café, leaving Nick behind to converse with Rodriguez in Tagalog.

Nick caught up with me in the lobby. As we rode back to his house, I simmered in silent anger. Halfway there, I finally asked, "What did you say to that bastard after I left?"

"I told him we would leave tomorrow, provided he agreed to certain conditions," he answered.

In disbelief, I asked, "What conditions?"

"In Filipino, we call it Panero. It essentially means two men of equal standing agreeing to keep their word."

"So, some sort of pledge?" I questioned.

"Yes, something like that," he replied.

"Kitty can provide her sworn testimony from Australia via proxy, and that should be enough to put those bastards behind bars for good. So, I guess it doesn't really matter if he escapes his involvement," I conceded, though the thought left a bitter taste in my mouth.

"At the end of the day, it's up to Kitty whether she wants to implicate Mayor Rodriguez or not," he said, a smug smile playing on his lips.

His implication dawned on me. Regardless of the path taken, Raye and Gutierrez would pay dearly for their crimes. If that meant keeping Kitty and ourselves safe while still achieving the desired result, I was all for it.

~ ~ ~

Later that afternoon, a helicopter touched down on the helipad in Nick's backyard. Dom accompanied me for a trip around Legazpi City. The four-hundred-kilometre flight took around ninety minutes, and the views throughout were absolutely mesmerising. As we neared

Legazpi airport, the pilot gave us an incredible view of Mount Mayon, an active volcano. It was a breathtaking sight.

A car awaited us at the airport. Dom hopped into the driver's seat, and we embarked on our journey to Magnolia Street. I marvelled at Nick's meticulous planning; everything moved with the precision of a Patek Philippe watch.

Twenty minutes later, we arrived at an old house at the end of a humble suburban street. The houses around us clearly belonged to the less fortunate.

"This is it, sir," Dom announced.

"Dom, I could use your help in case they don't speak English," I said, preparing to exit the car.

The house was in a dilapidated state, with chickens pecking about on the front lawn. We navigated past them, trudging through waist-high weeds to the front door, where we knocked. An elderly lady eventually answered. Dom spoke to her in Tagalog, and she responded with a toothless smile, inviting us to sit with her on the porch. I suspected that I was her first foreign visitor, given the attention she directed at me.

I instructed Dom to gently explain that, following the tragedy that befell Chiki, I wished to meet her son, Carlo. She nodded and called out his name. A shy, handsome young boy emerged from the house, taking a seat next to his grandmother. I reached out to shake his hand. He hesitated but then extended his hand as well.

"Hi Carlo, I'm Axis."

"Hi Axis," he mumbled, slightly uncertain about his English.

I retrieved an envelope from my back pocket and handed it to him. "Your mom wanted you to have this, son. She wanted you to go to a good school."

Carlo cautiously accepted the envelope, peering inside. His eyes widened in surprise, and he handed it to his grandmother. Upon seeing the contents, she burst into tears and began speaking rapidly to Dom in Tagalog.

Dom translated for me. "Sir, Irene says this is the most money she has ever seen. She believes you are an angel sent by God to bring this gift to Carlo. This money will provide him with opportunities in life, and he will never forget you."

I gave Irene my business card and promised, "When Carlo grows up, he can contact me. I will always be there to help."

Dom relayed the message to them. Irene and Carlo stood up and hugged me. Despite the sorrow of losing his mother, Carlo's face radiated hope. The sight made the visit entirely worthwhile.

I found myself fighting back tears as I said goodbye to Carlo and his loving grandmother.

~ ~ ~

Saying goodbye to Nick at Ninoy Aquino International Airport felt like parting from a close friend. Despite our differences and arguments, we'd endured a lot together, creating a bond that would last a lifetime. We planned to meet in Sydney, after he'd followed Kitty and Lola to Brisbane. But for the moment, we had to leave him behind as we boarded a Qantas flight bound for Sydney, with a stop in Brisbane.

As we left Nick at the departure gate, Kitty became a picture of grief, leaning on Lola for support.

On the plane, Lola and I sat together, with Kitty across the aisle. Once we were airborne and the seatbelt sign turned off, the business-class hostess offered me a selection of newspapers. I picked the Philippine Star. Opening it, I found a shocking headline on page three: "Ringo Raye and Arnel Gutierrez Killed in Police Vehicle Accident." The article reported that the two men, accused of kidnapping and murder, were being transferred between prisons when the tragedy happened. A truck ran a red light and collided with their police van, which then caught fire. The truck driver and the two policemen in the van escaped unharmed, but Raye and Gutierrez, handcuffed in the back of the van, perished in the blaze. It would have been a gruesome death.

Suddenly, the meaning of 'Panero' and the agreement between Nick and Mayor Rodriguez became clear. This was how it had to happen—a safe exit for the mayor, and closure for the case. It even crossed my mind that this could have been another of Nick's meticulously planned operations. The mayor had said that every country's law ultimately administers justice, but I couldn't help hoping that if karma existed, the mayor would meet his reckoning one day.

Showing Lola the article, she merely smiled and said, without much emotion, "Huh, what goes around comes around." When Kitty read the news, we both observed her sink into her seat with a profound sense of relief.

~ ~ ~

I bid the girls goodbye at Brisbane airport and settled into the transit lounge, my mind filled with memories of my suicide blonde and all the fascinating experiences we'd shared. Pulling out my smartphone, I turned off the roaming feature and switched my ringtone from The Terrible Tango to another favourite of mine, Someday Soon. It had become a tradition of mine to select a different ringtone for each case, and I was optimistic that a new one awaited me in Sydney. Just as I finished changing my settings, a call for the boarding of flight QF20 to Sydney came over the PA system.

As the large Qantas jet ascended, we punched through the dense, gloomy clouds that blanketed Brisbane like an unwelcome hangover. After a bit of turbulence, we emerged into the serenity of a clear blue dawn sky—a sensation I cherished as it symbolised for me the onset of a fresh, exciting adventure.

The End

Stay tuned for the next Axis Stone Mystery in book two,

LEG MAN

www.ingramcontent.com/pod-product-compliance
Lightning Source LLC
Chambersburg PA
CBHW052019030426

42335CB00026B/3205